Also by George Boelcke:

Keeping Your Money

**Colorful Personalities: Discover your personality type
through the power of Colors**
(www.vantageseminars.com)

The Colors of Leadership and Management

The Colors of Parent & Child Dynamics

The Colors of Relationships

The Stories of Colors

The Colors of Customers and Sales

It's Your Money!

*Tools, tips & tricks
to borrow smarter
and pay it off quicker*

Vantage Publishing
Suite 1183 – 14781 Memorial Drive, Houston, TX 77079
Web site: www.yourmoneybook.com
E-mail: sales@yourmoneybook.com

This book and the information contained herein is intended as a general guide, and as educational material only. The author assumes no responsibility for errors, omissions, inaccuracies or any inconsistency herein and makes no promises or claims regarding the application or use. It is sold with the understanding that neither the publisher nor the author is rendering legal, financial, accounting or professional services. The reader should always consult a financial professional for specific application to all individual situations. While great care has been taken in the preparation of all reference charts, they are a guide only and are rounded to the nearest dollar. Specific payments should be obtained from the company you are dealing with.

Cover & design assistance: David Macpherson
Edited by: Veniece Tedeschini & Crystal Lidgren
Layout & typeset by: Ingénieuse Productions, Edmonton

FIRST EDITION

Printed in the United States of America

National Library of Canadian Cataloguing in Publication

Boelcke, George J., 1959–
         It's Your Money! Tools, tips & tricks to borrow smarter and pay it off quicker / George J. Boelcke.

Includes index.
ISBN 0-9736668-0-3

         Consumer credit. 2. Finance, Personal I.Title.

HG3701.B63 2004   332.024   C2004-902725-5.

It's Your Money!

Tools, tips & tricks
to borrow smarter
and pay it off quicker

An invaluable Reference Guide

A must-read for every American

George J. Boelcke, F.C.I.

Contents

Introduction

Why You Need to Know

Credit – love it or hate it – almost all of use it and most of us can't live without it. Unfortunately, most of us also don't understand it very well and that costs us dearly in the added interest we pay and total debt we accumulate.

This book should become your best friend, and be your insider guide into many areas of credit. Having a basic insider knowledge of credit is an invaluable resource for getting credit, keeping it and then getting rid of the debt it can bring as fast as possible. Plus, you'll understand your options. Anyone uninformed, in a hurry, unwilling to ask questions or easily intimidated will never obtain the best deal for themselves. Let's face it, nobody has a vested interest in explaining shortcuts, savings or options to you.

Understanding the ins and outs of financing is a mystery to most people. There is seldom a black or white answer and credit decisions are not mathematical equations with clear or tidy explanations. Credit decisions are as unique as the people applying, and sometimes that's very confusing. In the time it takes just to read the next page:

- Dozens of Americans will be filing for bankruptcy.

- Hundreds are signing mortgage loans trusting, but not really knowing, what their rights, costs, or interest charges really are.

- Thousands will be buying consumer goods on credit without knowing all the facts of what they're signing.

- Tens of thousands are charging away on their credit cards hoping, but not certain, to make more than a minimum payment next month.

- Hundreds of thousands are making payments on the purchase or lease of an automobile on terms that might have seemed a good idea at the time.

- Millions of individuals are carrying more than one credit card in their wallet and treating it as cash, with many potential pitfalls.

Every day, countless numbers of consumers make poor or uninformed credit decisions that create consequences for years to come. It is never by choice, but because they don't know the credit tricks or pitfalls, or the right questions to ask first.

The greatest asset you have is to ask questions—the right questions.

How did we get here and how do we avoid some of these expensive traps? It will be through understanding the inside rules and tips of credit - *how to get it* – in the least costly way. It is also through managing debt – *the how to get rid of it* part.

Obtaining credit is not a gift or a windfall as it only creates spending power for today. The downside is that repayment must be made at some point. This results in spending more money later when interest charges are added to make up for the *gotta have it today* attitude. So, credit always comes at a cost of future purchasing power when the bills arrive. When you're making payments on last year's stuff, you're using up a lot of money that can't be saved or put toward this year's stuff.

This book is not about numbers – they are deliberately kept to a minimum. Even all examples are rounded to the nearest dollar. Plus, nobody expects you to read this book from beginning to end, but it will become an invaluable reference guide. You'll see many examples of ways you've borrowed without always knowing what's really happening with long forms, tiny print or pushy salespeople in your face. Chances are you might not have known what to look for, or to avoid, and anyway – who wants to look or feel stupid? Next time, you'll be ready – with some tools, knowledge and the right questions to ask. After all, if you don't ask, nobody will, as others won't be making your payments or helping you pay your debts later.

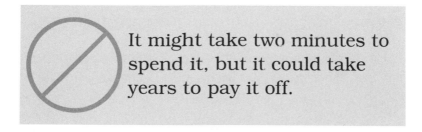

It might take two minutes to spend it, but it could take years to pay it off.

According to the Federal Reserve, more than 40 percent of Americans spend more each month than they earn – and it's rising. At the same time, our savings rate keeps dropping and has now gone down to almost one percent of after tax income. That's seven times less than it was just 20 years ago – ouch! For most of us it'll be years before we see the light at the end of the tunnel. More and more borrowing, with an increasing debt load, and almost no cushion of savings to fall back on is not a good combination. So for many, being debt-free is quite an unrealistic goal for the foreseeable future and many are just a paycheck or two away from serious financial problems.

Chapter 1

The Start of Credit

Credit has been around for centuries. The word comes from the Latin credo meaning *belief*, or simply put, I trust. Documents date back to around 1800 BC when the King of Babylon referred to the granting of loans and punishment for any non-payment. The concept of interest came from Roman law and simply reasoned that charging interest (extra charges for making the loan) was a fair return to lenders.

Credit is broadly classified into two main areas. The first category is mercantile trade, which involves credit between businesses. In this field, being able to get credit is almost mandatory. Very few businesses could survive on a cash basis in their dealings with suppliers, customers or wholesalers. It has always been accepted that over 90 percent of transactions between businesses involve credit in some way.

Consumer credit is the same principle, but applied to individuals. It ranges from mortgages to credit cards, personal loans and lines of credit to overdrafts and pawnbrokers. It allows consumers the chance to buy now - pay later. Often a very tempting idea, but it comes with the responsibility of some planning and budgeting and can make the word credit misleading – perhaps the proper term should be taking on debt.

The other common theme is that most consumer credit involves borrowing for consumption, whether it's charging a meal, a new wardrobe, or borrowing to finance a boat or vacation. In all cases, the item is consumed or depreciates (reduces) in value. In other words, it is used up, gone or worth less down the road. That is quite different from credit obtained for investments, IRAs, a 401 (k) or some asset that increases in value over time and where interest may even be tax deductible. That is actually borrowing money to make money.

The first widespread use of consumer credit was started by Singer Sewing Machines. Their marketing was directed at women, who in that era were almost exclusively housewives. Selling sewing machines to them presented a problem, as the women were unable to afford it since they didn't possess much of their own discretionary income. Singer overcame this by creating a sale with a partial down payment and the balance paid over a number of months on affordable terms.

Since the Second World War consumer credit has exploded and evolved significantly. It has played a huge part in the growth of the entire economy and has created higher standards of living. Things such as credit cards and personal credit lines, as well as overall reductions in the amount of down payments, have all left their mark. Some for the better – some for the worse.

Is credit really necessary or is it wiser to always pay cash? If the enjoyment of having something today through financing outweighs the cost, to that person it's worth it. However, it is quite normal to exaggerate the need at the moment, while often ignoring the cost or implications for the future.

 Using credit might be convenient, but it always comes at a price. Whether that cost is worth paying only you can decide.

In spite of the natural tendency to downplay debts, credit sales drive a large part of today's economy. Credit allows individuals to enjoy a high standard of living and is essential to the operation of governments and all companies. Credit is also a field of constant changes and demands, and has evolved into computerized credit checks, instant approvals, automated collection systems and a simple numerical FICO score to judge the odds of lenders being paid back.

Chapter 2

Credit 101

 Credit is something you must be able to manage well and use to your advantage— not just as a convenience.

Obtaining credit is not a right but an earned privilege to be able to use the money of others. It involves the exchange or sale of goods and services for the promise to pay it back over a period of time and involves two main elements:

- Future – The time frame until the repayment is due or the length of time the money is owed.
- Risk – The chances of being paid back within a certain time as agreed to or being paid back when the loan is due.

Both of these elements are what lenders use to calculate how much interest to charge, how long the term is and how much risk there is in getting paid back. After the loan is made, the debt has to be repaid. If this doesn't happen, many will suffer to various degrees. Default on a credit card can impact all cardholders at some point through higher interest rates. On the other extreme, non-payment by large corporations or a developing nation has a much larger effect throughout the economy.

Credit in everyday life can mean that $10 lent to a friend for a day is a small amount and relatively risk free. Another safe bet is $200 lent for a week while holding a $700 watch, since the collateral is more valuable than the loan. Borrowing in a more formal way from a financial institution operates in much the same way. A mortgage with a house as security will always have a lower interest rate than a finance company loan with or without collateral.

Credit and a credit rating is almost a necessity nowadays, as society continues evolving to become more and more cashless. No, not everyone has to have a credit card, or even wants one, but those people are few and far between. Without some form of plastic in your wallet, some lifestyle adjustments or inconveniences may be necessary.

It is very difficult to find anyone that doesn't rely on credit in one way or another. Even those who say they only deal in cash actually deal with a form of credit. Since the abandonment of the gold standard, governments across the world continue to print money that they have to make good on. This paper currency incurs debt for the government, so paper money is also a form of credit. Another is simply having a bank account. The depositor is really extending credit to the financial institution. It is a debt that has to be paid back to the depositor when the money is withdrawn. Financial institutions simply take the deposits of customers and recycle them by lending this same money out through loans, mortgages and other forms of credit. They pay interest to customers with deposits and savings, while collecting fees and interest from lending out the money to others at a higher rate.

The What and How of Credit

Today's society, for better or worse, almost mandates having a credit rating of some kind. Seldom, if ever, will a car rental company release a vehicle without a major credit card and even just reserving a hotel room can be a challenge without one.

Obtaining credit is largely based on your past track record. Since someone is selling you credit in the hope of getting it back, it is their choice to say yes or no. Your option in the transaction is to shop around for the best terms, lowest rate and most favorable arrangements. The two goals for financial institutions are to lend out money at a profit and to be certain they get paid back. Large numbers of people think that creditors have a crystal ball and should be able to see that *things are great now* that *they should take a chance on me.* Simply put – it doesn't work like that.

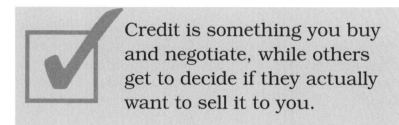

Credit is something you buy and negotiate, while others get to decide if they actually want to sell it to you.

What was the last big-ticket item you purchased? A computer, car or maybe some furniture? Perhaps you checked a couple of ads or a few stores to find the best deal. You weren't always looking for the least expensive one, but probably a combination of features and price. That same comparison-shopping when it comes to credit could save you hundreds or thousands of dollars. Even a relatively small $100,000 mortgage over 30 years can save you around $4,600 if you are able to find a rate just one-quarter percent lower. Isn't that a worthwhile investment of time as well?

Payday Loans and Short-term Credit Traps

It is estimated that between one-quarter and one-third of the population has challenges getting credit for one reason or another. The main ones include lack of income, credit problems, total debts, or people who have simply fallen through the credit scoring cracks, have never fought back and just gave up. A large group of these customers find that a lack of job stability or minimal income, both of which are often related, make obtaining credit almost impossible. Almost 13 percent of families don't even have a bank account according to the Federal Reserve. One of their few sources of credit tends to be lay-away plans where merchants dictate the terms and obtaining the item takes quite some time. Another option is often the short-term credit industry. In all cases, the majority of lower income, or marginal applicants do get treated noticeably worse. When credit is granted the prices and/or rates will almost always be higher than those available to other customers.

Every day there are ads promoting short-term borrowing until next payday. Unfortunately, these are very expensive and are almost exclusively targeted at consumers with credit problems or the working poor. While it may sound easy, there are large fees and interest charges to pay for the convenience. This industry includes payday loan companies, rent to own stores, pawn shops, title loan companies and other check-cashing operations. Many will advance up to 30 percent of an individual's net pay until the next payday. This does come at a price – a very high price of advancing $80 for a $100 payment in two weeks. Federal law considers 36 percent rates the maximum before being called extortion, but these types of industries don't consider their transactions as loans. They call check cashing a service, payday loans a deferred deposit, rent to own a lease, and title pawns an advance.

Their main business is a one-time repayment instead of a typical monthly payment plan. Customers leave a post-dated check or sign an automatic bank withdrawal for repayment on their next payday. Not being able to pay often leads to rolling over their debt by continuously arranging new advances to repay older ones in an effort to avoid NSF charges, frequently with no end in sight. With vast numbers of operations, it is a highly competitive field. Their success is due to customers who are not well informed and the terms are not easily understood to an average borrower. They are the fastest growing segment of alternative financing but not uniformly regulated in all States. Rent to own places target poorer clients whose consumer dreams would not otherwise be possible. But the total interest on an item can often exceed two or three hundred percent when something is re-leased or rented numerous times after returns or repossessions are factored in.

Unfortunately these individuals often have nowhere else to turn for their financial needs. A study some years ago by the Federal Trade Commission showed that 73 percent of second tier finance customers had a high school education or less and 60 percent had incomes under $25,000. Sadly, this also includes vast numbers of African Americans and Hispanic Americans, whose income and assets continue to lag below the national average. It should make educating these groups on credit, debt, ways to become homeowners and savings tools one of the biggest national priorities – which will also have one of the biggest payoffs for the country as a whole in measurable ways.

Getting Started For First-Time Borrowers

Yes, there are individuals who have never borrowed and have never desired a credit card. This is a small minority, generally older people, not raised with the concept of borrowing for any reason. How sad that this is something few people can accomplish these days. Today, prices in relation to income earned make it almost impossible to obtain certain things without some form of credit.

The underlying premise for credit decisions is a credit rating. Only by judging how another account has been paid in the past can any decision be made with any degree of accuracy about the future. To make matters harder to understand, the previous amount borrowed enters into this consideration as well. It is referred to as high credit and is a factor in almost all decisions. In simple terms, it means that someone with a department store credit card and a limit of $500 will not be successful in obtaining a $10,000 loan. The jump is simply too large to borrow 20 times more than before.

Credit is granted when the applicant has a good payment history. A good applicant is someone without excessive debt and the ability to repay the amount borrowed. This makes it important to establish a credit rating immediately upon reaching legal age. Learning about credit as a tool and a resource should not be something that is avoided until absolutely necessary. For better or worse, it is an integral part of today's society. And yes, building up credit can cost fees and interest charges. Paying some of these is a worthwhile investment in building a solid credit foundation. Any teen that has been taught at home about credit, both the pitfalls and benefits, will more likely be responsible and educated enough to ask good questions and take the right steps to successfully manage credit well during their lifetime.

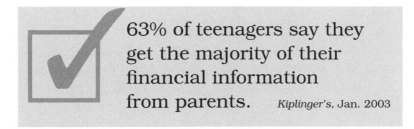

63% of teenagers say they get the majority of their financial information from parents. *Kiplinger's*, Jan. 2003

There are many ways for first time borrowers to establish credit. These are all based on the assumption that the applicant is employed, has sufficient income to repay the loan, is of legal age and has had no previous credit problems. Having no credit is still better than bad credit.

• Department store cards – These will generally be approved for first time applicants with a modest credit limit. It may not be much, but it's an excellent start. They are relatively easy to obtain as the merchant uses their in-house cards to attract customers. At the same time, it creates a loyal client for them and increases repeat business.

• IRA loan (Individual Retirement Account) - Yes, this does count as a real loan, and often at very attractive rates. In return, the IRA stays in the control of the lender until the loan is paid in full. This is an excellent way, with very little interest, to create a win-win situation of establishing credit and saving taxes, while building savings for retirement. It usually needs to be over a 12-month term and only applies to people who qualify for an IRA in the first place.

• Cosigner – This is the most common first loan for young people. A cosigner is someone that signs along with the applicant. That person becomes as equally responsible for the repayment as the actual borrower. That is why lenders tend to require a family member, so it should always be considered as a last resort. Often a smaller loan or an increased down payment can eliminate the need for a cosigner. After all, would a family member prefer to lend someone an additional down payment or sign for the entire length of the loan?

- Car loan – Assuming it's a reasonably priced used vehicle, a 30 to 50 percent down payment through a reputable dealer might secure financing without a cosigner. The loan should be structured to shorten the term or increase the down payment – both of which reduce risk. Vehicles usually need to be less than seven years old to qualify for reasonable rates.

- New vehicle lease - For a first time purchaser this is also a possible option. A lease allows the lender to only advance the amount of the vehicle, since taxes are not charged up front. For these, some manufacturers even have a special credit process for first time borrowers or post secondary student. It won't be a Cadillac, and a larger down payment will be necessary.

- Secured Visa or MasterCard - Many financial institutions issue these specialized credit cards. Secured simply means a cash deposit in the amount of the credit limit is placed on deposit as collateral against any potential non-payment. Other than this deposit, the card looks and charges exactly the same and also comes with the usual late and over limit fees like all other cards. The deposit stays in place until the credit card is closed or changed to a regular account. This is an excellent method of obtaining good credit references after 18-24 months.

- Loans secured with savings or a certificate of deposit - Any loan that is fully secured this way is fairly easy to obtain, up to 80 or 90 percent of the total amount. Would you lend someone $90 if they gave you $100 to hold as collateral? Of course - sounds stupid? - not really. The certificate of deposit may be locked in or attract interest penalties if cashed early. Besides, a little interest paid on a loan while getting most of it back on the certificate of deposit is a worthwhile investment and an easy solution to build a good basic credit rating.

• Student credit cards - For years now, card companies have aggressively marketed to college or university students. Some even claim "Applying for a Visa Card is as easy as writing your own name. You don't need a cosigner. You don't need a job. After all, being a student is your job." What is the reason they're prepared to do this? Studies show that three out of four college students stay loyal to their first card for more than 15 years. Besides, card issuers have 25 or 30 percent new clients each September as freshmen enter college and university.

They are relatively easy to obtain and establish the foundation of a good credit rating. Sixty five percent of students do have a credit card, but their average balance is already over $2,000.

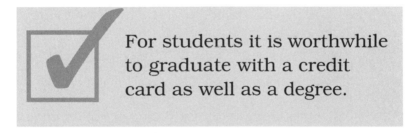

For students it is worthwhile to graduate with a credit card as well as a degree.

All of these options have some basic common denominators. The credit extended is of a relatively modest amount, or has a large down payment. Secondly, the lender may have good collateral for the loan. This is done either by holding collateral in cash, savings, certificate of deposit, or through a large equity percentage in something like a vehicle because of the down payment. All of these reduce any risk to the credit grantor since nobody is likely to walk away from that type of arrangement.

Since these general suggestions are designed to build credit, it is important to specifically ask if the lender reports their loans automatically and by computer to the credit bureaus. This will ensure actually receiving the benefit of a credit rating. It is not worth the risk if a lender promises to manually report the information. It likely won't happen and there are many other lenders who will report directly.

Chapter 3

Credit Cards

 Research shows over and over that consumers spend more on a credit card than they would with cash— always.

Credit cards were really developed at the start of the century when some innkeepers started to issue identification cards to their regular clients. They were used to check in and out, and allowed billing of charges by mail, after the client had left. It's ironic that today without one of these now called credit cards, the chances of obtaining a room are next to none.

The first card useable at more than one establishment was Diner's Club, designed in the early 1950s, exclusively for restaurants. Frank McNamara, the creator, signed up less than 100 members from his first mailer, but two years later was billing out over one million dollars and the credit card business was firmly established forever. Talk about a concept that was quickly accepted and is here to stay. Back then, as is the case today, any personal touch was already long gone. The rows of computers with billions of transactions and hundreds of millions of accounts made each cardholder simply a number – a long number – and one of very many. But with the massive costs of setting up and administering a credit card program, plus a learning curve that caused millions of dollars in write-offs, it became obvious in the late 1960s that only two companies of any size would survive. They removed any talk in ads about charge or debit, Chargex became Visa, MasterCharge became MasterCard, and both started to evolve into financial services companies instead of simple credit card issuers.

At first, banks actually had little interest in credit cards, but processing billions of checks became very expensive. There were also over a dozen steps for the banks that ranged from accepting them to the eventual return with the customer's statement and all the necessary handling in between. This inefficient system cost the banks many millions of dollars in administration costs, not all of which they could hope to recover from customers through service charges.

Credit cards became their bridge from the use of checks, to their eventual goal of total electronic banking. It was a training ground for customers to convert them from using checks to using little plastic cards. Plus, they were getting into a fast growing area that was becoming very lucrative and easy for them to compete in because of their large client base. It wasn't that hard to sell, and all that remained was some marketing which has been very effective. In the last few decades, their ad campaigns have certainly changed our view of money, cash, debt and necessities.

Actual credit card marketing is really just a numbers game. The more people apply, the more are approved, and the more they will carry big balances and pay interest each month. That's why it's hard to walk from one end of a mall to another without being pitched that just filling out an application can get you a free T-shirt or other gift. Almost any conventional lending requires collateral of some kind or another. Not so if someone can simply use three or four credit cards that may easily add up to 10 or 20 thousand dollars of unsecured debt – for anything at any time. How many cards are too many? At one point, Walter Cavanagh certainly had the record with over 1,300 valid cards. Yes, he was rejected once – only once, when a store suggested he already had a sufficient number. You think?

One of the strangest stories of living on credit cards certainly belongs to Director Richard Linklater. He financed his first film, *Slacker*, using every dime of credit limits on a number of his cards. "I made *Slacker* with two Visas, two MasterCards and a Sears card", confessed Linklater. Sad, but true – yet how many use their Visa to pay their MasterCard when money is tight?

 Unfortunately a frequently heard comment is: "I can't afford it, so I'll just put it on my credit card."

Right now there are more than one billion cards in consumer's wallets. That means the average household has more than nine cards, a figure that has more than doubled over the past five years. In fact, over 80 percent of Americans have at least one card. It has become the sad reality that credit cards can seem more valuable than cash. Small wonder that Visa and MasterCard are used for over 1.5 trillion dollars in purchases a year.

There are over 6,000 different Visa and MasterCards alone, marketed by thousands of companies. Banks, independent financial institutions, credit unions, community banks and many others issue them. All of which can be used at millions of places in the country and around the world. Consumers can now even pay groceries and phone bills with their credit card.

Most other borrowing requires repayment in a fixed manner over a specific term. Quite the opposite is true with credit cards. Statistics show that only 37 percent of major credit card holders pay their balance in full by the due date. If not, issuers can tack on interest charges usually ranging from 10 to 23 percent for almost two-thirds of all accounts that carry a balance at the end of the month. It's a sad day for the companies when their customers do pay off their balance. To avoid this as long as possible, even the minimum payments have now been reduced by many companies to as low as two percent per month.

"The card was never intended to encourage
people to spend beyond their means."
Joe Titus – First Credit Manager of The Diners Club (1959)

A better quote came from a past Visa USA President, Dee Hock: *"People don't suddenly get dumb because we give them a piece of plastic."* Well, Mr. Hock – maybe not permanently dumb, but sometimes...

Card Categories

Credit cards are identified by four main categories:

• Major cards (also called bank cards) include Visa, MasterCard and American Express, which are very extensive in their usage, quantity in circulation and general acceptance not only in North America, but worldwide.

American Express does have many cards that operate differently than other major cards. Their billing system requires the balance to be paid by the due date. These cards are referred to as charge cards, not credit cards, since they must be paid in full with each statement.

• Affinity cards: These are cards issued together with non-profit organizations, colleges, animal and environmental groups, or any causes that have their name and logo on the cards. When the credit card is used, a portion of the merchant fee goes to support that group or cause, generally one-half of one percent at most. That means $100 charged gives about 50 cents to the organization. As they compete with other cards, their rates, fees and costs will generally be competitive.

Issuers love nothing more than loyal clients that can care more about their minimal donation than the interest rate on their card. Plus the credit card company gets access to the mailing lists of the organization for their marketing, and access to a whole new group of potential clients. Considering the image most people have of credit card companies, this is an area where they can actually look like good guys.

• Co-branded cards: These are issued for specific companies and linked with that retail partner. These create a tie-in between the card and the merchant, which is designed to keep their customers loyal. The tie-ins generally include points or rebates toward products of that merchant. General Motors, for example, has their tie-in with Household Bank for their MasterCard, with the opportunity to earn rebates of five percent toward the purchase or lease of a new vehicle. In fact, when the card was introduced, over three million cardholders were signed up in the first few months. In the first five years of the GM program launch, customers had already collected close to one billion dollars in rebates, even with annual limits on accumulations.

Sometimes these cards are also called dual cards. They are actually issued by Visa or MasterCard for a specific merchant, whose name is on the card, but can also be used like a regular credit card everywhere else. They are governed by Federal Banking laws with stricter State consumer protection on late fees, interest charges and other areas. To avoid some of these restrictive laws, many cards are issued in States that have much more relaxed consumer protection laws, such as Delaware and South Dakota. You'll know, because that's where you will be sending your payments. You may live in California, but the rules apply to the State where the card is issued, not where you live.

Some of the latest ones? E-Bay now has a co-branded card with MBNA to earn points toward purchases on their Web site. Also now available is a Disney Visa card and a Starbucks card, both issued by Bank One, and even a Tiger Woods America Express card.

- Store or retail cards – these include everything from gas stations to department store chains, stereo stores and furniture retailers to name a few. These are convenience charge cards to encourage loyalty to certain stores or chains ranging from Staples and Eddie Bauer to Macy's and Gulf Oil. Since they are restricted to the issuing merchant, they are very limiting, but encourage customer loyalty to a certain retailer. These cards are either operated by the company directly or administered by large national credit card management firms.

Gift Cards

Gift cards are the most recent invention of credit card issuers and retail stores to keep growing and increasing their bottom line. A gift card is actually a gift certificate for a fixed prepaid amount of generally $25 to $750, which is loaded onto a credit card. It can then be used over and over again until the prepaid amount is used up, and many can even be reloaded for more money. Their popularity is exploding and volumes already exceed $50 billion. Stores market these instead of gift certificates, as it is a lot less hassle and paperwork for them, while credit card issuers market their unrestricted use.

But would you pay admission to get into a mall? Many gift cards do come with a set-up or activation fee ranging from $5 to $12. Many also expire, or have a monthly inactivity or dormancy fee of around $2.50, which can kick in after as little as six months. Others even prohibit purchasing anything higher than the available credit. Small wonder consumer groups are concerned about their lack of regulations. As with everything else, it's buyer beware, read the details with the gift card, ask the right questions and use it up. Around 12 percent of gift cards are never even redeemed, resulting in over six billion dollars of profit for the issuers.

Convenience Checks

Convenience checks come with every credit card. They are checks to allow instant access up to the full credit limit. It is a quick way for the issuer to get customers closer to their maximum limit. This is something that would take a lot longer if it could only be done through normal charges. They are first sent out with the intent of getting customers to transfer other balances over to the new card. That may be the case, but it also allows customers to play a shell game between credit cards by using one to pay another. Plus, these original balance transfers can sometimes be treated as cash advances. The fine print will disclose that this could mean no interest-free period, often at a higher rate, and they may not qualify for any introductory rate.

 People with debt problems often blame credit cards. But isn't the real issue poor money management?

Credit card debt can become a mortgage for life, especially with cash advances and access to convenience checks. Interest on advances also has no grace period and starts immediately. On top of that, many companies charge around two to four percent of the advance, and a minimum fee, which can be $15 or more for each cash-advance. In fact, Visa alone has cash volumes of almost $300 billion each year. But again, it is your option to stop the cash withdrawal feature on any card. It just takes a little discipline and a two-minute telephone call.

Credit Limits

All credit cards come with a pre-set spending maximum called the credit limit. It is the highest amount of money the card issuer is prepared to advance. Just as joint bank accounts have only one balance, credit cards have only one actual limit. No matter how many physical cards are linked to a dependent or spouse, the limit exists for all cards together. As there is only a single account, these supplemental cards as they are called, are the same account with different names. There is only one billing (plus one credit rating for the actual cardholder only) and one spending limit.

Once every year or two, it is likely there will be an increase in your credit limit. This might be flattering, but they're trying to get you to load up enough of a balance where the hangover will last past the grace period. In other words - where the balance is not paid in full. With more than 63 percent of all customers, that's already happening. They still want to get paid back - just not very fast. There is still the annual fee for most, but they'd rather charge you interest as well.

Out of money? Stop spending! But with any number of cards and high limits, where is the reason or incentive to stop?

Why Credit Limits Change

After setting an initial credit limit, the card issuer has no obligation to ever raise this amount. They can leave the limit, lower it or increase it. However, companies do adjust limits from time-to-time. The credit card field is very competitive with each company fighting not only for market share, but to keep their well paying accounts loyal and happy. It is, as in any business, less costly to retain a customer than to attract a new one.

Credit limits are not set in stone. The issuer bases the initial limit on the original application. The amount is set by the issuer, based on their investigation and consists mainly of the credit bureau report and current debt calculations. But since the issuer has not updated the credit application, (nobody has called you to update any information) how did the credit limit get adjusted?

This is accomplished through periodic updates of your credit report and something called behavior scoring. In simple terms, it deals with the conduct of the cardholder and can adjust credit limits based on this information. It is done through the use of sophisticated computers and vast amounts of past data on each account. A portion of this system reviews the usual amount of each charge. While the national average is $82, customers use them in different ways. The company's analysis can include information ranging from the number of charges each month, the per transaction amount, or average unpaid balance. It can also gather information from each transaction regarding the type of purchases and much more. When this is included, it allows a certain degree of tailoring credit limits to client needs.

Having card activity history available is not only good service to the client, but also good marketing and monitoring. The data is held in strictest confidence and is never disclosed to any outside party, but used purely for internal purposes. This information is also very valuable for fraud protection. With this information, card issuers can quickly detect unusual charge activity where patterns have suddenly changed on an account.

Each customer has a fair amount of control over his or her card limit. It is simply a matter of contacting the financial institution to request an increase. On the other hand, a customer can also decline a credit limit raise, or simply instruct to have it lowered. Not all people should have a growing credit limit. But very few take this step, and it can be a great idea for people that:

• Have previously consolidated credit card balances into a loan when the balance got carried away or unmanageable, if the card has not been returned already or the account closed.

• Are not sure they can trust themselves to avoid running their card to the limit.

• Claim they only have it for identification or emergency use.

• Recognize that any credit card, and high credit limits, are not status symbols. It is simply a convenience card used only for what can be paid in full by the due date every month.

Taking the step of reducing a limit is not a sign of a problem, or derogatory in any way, but often just wise credit management.

Annual Fees

In the early 1980s, inflation was almost 20 percent and interest rates went up right along with it. President Carter and the Federal Reserve wanted to shift some of the blame to banks for rising rates. To slow the use of credit cards, they implemented a nine-percent growth rate limit. Since banks had no desire to slow profits, they began charging an annual fee. To them, even if 10 percent of customers canceled, they were still collecting millions of dollars for doing nothing extra. From that point on, while perks may have been added, annual fees were here to stay.

Every credit card accomplishes their basic purpose. After that, it comes down to an individual decision of finding the most attractive rate (not just the promotional rate), choice of features, benefits, points or perks. It is a competitive field, so it always pays to shop around since programs can certainly be amended, and rates or annual fees can change. As a rule of thumb, cards with fees generally include more features. But then it is always wiser to decide why you are getting the card in the first place.

The Free Grace Period

The grace period is the length of time from the date of your statement until you have to make a payment or pay the balance in full. This due date is not *about* or *close to*, it is actually outlined to the exact hour and date on each statement. Plus it starts with the statement date and not the date it is mailed, or the date received in your mailbox.

On partial payments, interest on purchases start retroactive to day one if the entire balance is not paid. If the statement is paid in full, there will never be an interest charge. The grace periods can range from a couple of weeks to a month, and varies with each issuer. It should be one of many considerations when shopping for a card, as this free time can vary by up to two weeks. Card issuers are certainly making their best efforts to reduce this free time little by little. After all, the shorter the free ride, the quicker they can start charging interest. For cash advances or convenience checks, interest always starts from the date you take out the funds, along with their fees – they are treated as a loan and have no interest-free period.

Does your free time stop just short of payday? This can be very expensive and isn't well known to millions of cardholders. It means you will be charged interest at the end of the grace period for that full month, even if you pay one hour after the cut-off. So if you want the free time to go until your paycheck, contact your card issuer to change your statement date. One call could save you literally hundreds of dollars and a likely rate increase simply by adjusting your date.

It is also possible for many cards to have payment deducted automatically from your bank account, similar to a vehicle or mortgage loan, if your card is issued by your financial institution. You can choose the amount to be a minimum payment, a flat amount or the full balance to ensure that you will always avoid late charges and other fees. Or, you can set your card up for online payments with almost all cards.

Understanding Credit Card Interest

Picture a business with an unlimited supply of low cost product and a big profit margin. That's the essence of a credit card operation. Plus, they have millions of customers who carry a balance each month, many of whom pay the minimum payment to *avoid* the whole $2,000 balance. After all, a small $40 or $60 payment stalls off the balance for another month. With two or three percent payments at most, very little actually goes to the principal. Of course, when consumers take advantage of the lower monthly payment, the interest costs keep increasing. Very bad for the holder, but very good for the issuer.

 A $3000 balance on a typical card can take 17 years and over $3100 in interest to pay off.

At one point, the explanation of interest calculations was written in font maybe one-tenth of what you are reading here and was almost impossible to understand. Disclosure legislation has made finding, reading and understanding them much easier, but it can still be a challenge to find all the information on late charges, fees and rates, making comparison shopping very difficult. The Financial Consumer Agency commissioned a study in 2001 which found that more than 40 percent of cardholders actually didn't know the interest rate of their own cards.

Credit card issuers collect over $60 billion in interest charges each year, which doesn't include billions more in late fees, penalties or over limit charges. Unless your balance is paid off each month, there will be interest charges – and lots of them. Card companies have many different calculations to figure out your interest. The most widely used method is through the average daily balance.

Only a full payment of the balance avoids paying any interest. If not, leaving a balance of a penny or more will cost you another full month of interest on last months' balance. If the account has not reached zero, the payment you have made only counts toward the next month and interest is calculated for the entire last statement. Plus there are two ways a card issuer deals with an account balance. The difference can be very important and very expensive. Check your particular card:

Yes – you will still have a grace period on new charges – even though the meter is running on the old amount. It calculates interest on the average daily balance excluding new purchases.

 Careful! Some cards eliminate the free grace period entirely if there were any cash advances during the month.

No – once you haven't paid it in full, there is no free time ever on any charges until the balance is paid off and a new cycle starts. Their premise is you use it or lose it, so the average daily balance calculation already also includes new purchases.

Card issuers would really rather talk about perks, points and gifts than their rates. After all, any of those are a lot better for them than reducing their rates and giving up a whole lot of profit. But it never hurts to ask for a rate reduction. A study by the U.S. Public Interest Research Group had a range of clients call their card issuer to request a rate reduction. More than half actually received a lower rate just by asking. After all, if you don't ask – they won't volunteer it, but they sure want to keep their good clients, so it's always worth a telephone call.

An alternative could be to check out the credit cards issued by your local credit union or community bank. Their policies will be much more consumer-friendly, and your State's consumer laws regulate them. You'll also find fees and over-limit charges much lower and their payment deadlines more flexible.

 The general psychology is to forget the specific charges on our cards. Purchases are long forgotten—the debt all too real.

What Those Rates Really Mean

One of the best investments is always to pay off outstanding debt since the real cost is significantly higher than most people realize. It is only with actual take-home (after tax) pay that credit card interest can be paid. Someone with $2,000 to invest might be happy with a return of seven percent, which is $140 a year. Since interest can be taxed as income, even in the lowest tax bracket it reduces this amount even further.

How appealing would a totally risk free and guaranteed return of at least 22 percent be? Anyone with a credit card balance can have that return. To calculate the real cost of interest, simply take one minus the marginal tax rate, then take the rate of the card and divide it by that figure. For example:

1 – 0.25 (tax bracket) = 0.75. So a 19% credit card divided by this 0.75 is a 25.3% rate.

At a 19% card interest rate:		At a 28.8% card rate:
In a 15% tax bracket	22.4%	33.9%
In a 25% tax bracket	25.3%	38.4%
In a 30% tax bracket	27.1%	41.1%

After all, more than one dollar has to be earned to pay one dollar in debt after tax. It takes $1,334 in earnings just to pay off a $1,000 balance for someone with a 25 percent tax rate. That makes the best credit card balance no balance at all.

The Cheap Promotional Rate

Quite often, card issuers will mail out very attractive rate offers. Some even have a temporary zero percent teaser rate. Yes, a lower rate can translate into real savings, but only for a limited time. These offers vary, but generally have an attractive

 Promotional rates state in the fine print that it will revert back to regular rates if payment terms are not met.

promotional rate for only six months. It's always more important to read the details with a keen eye than focusing on the big headline. These rate promotions end immediately if the minimum payment is not made on time. After all, the card issuer is not trying to grow their arrears – they want good clients who always make their payments. During the promotional period, the issuer will encourage you to transfer balances from other accounts without transaction fees, but only during this time. Remember that they want your balance way up there when the promotional period ends and the real rate starts. In fact, the cool rate often only applies to transfers and not to regular charges.

If this is a new application and you want to switch your account, make sure to mark the end of the low rate period on your calendar and have a realistic plan to pay the account off before that date. If you are transferring other accounts to this temporary low rate, remember they will only be transferred after you are approved and only up to the maximum of your new credit limit. Do not assume your old bills are paid the day you're sending the application, but keep making payments until you confirm the transfers are posted through.

The Changing Fixed Credit Card Rates

For most people, the definition of a fixed rate is one that stays the same, such as a fixed mortgage rate. Well – this doesn't quite apply when it comes to credit card interest, which is really only fixed for a few weeks. Card issuers have to disclose how the rate will be calculated, but it is not their job to highlight this information for you. The Truth in Lending Act requires card issuers to supply 15 days notice before changing rates. Some States do require a longer notice period, but it is still a long way from calling it a fixed rate. It may be many years before a card issuer actually ups their rate for good customers, but the disclosure information always notes that this is possible with very little notice.

A variable rate card will fluctuate more often, although it will not generally be a large change month over month. They are based on or tied to an index (Treasury bill rate, Federal Reserve discount rate, federal funds rate, etc.), plus a percentage (the spread) depending on the creditworthiness of the customer.

Congratulations! You're Pre-Selected

Credit card companies work with a huge database of existing clients. A larger customer base means volume, and volume means profit in merchant discount charges and annual fees. More accounts also mean a larger group of cardholders that carry a balance on which interest charges are collected.

But attracting new cardholders is always a challenge. In Chicago during the mid-sixties, a number of issuers mailed out literally hundreds of thousands of actual unsolicited credit cards to names off almost any imaginable mailing list. It not only became a massively expensive lesson, but was also the end of mailing unsolicited credit cards.

Then for a number of years, marketing used a pre-approved letter that needed to be signed to issue a card. Today, more than 5.2 billion – yes, billion pre-approved solicitations are sent each year. With the natural hazards of pre-approvals, almost all mailings these days are instead pre-selected. While credit card issuers can get an advance look at your credit bureau report to target their mailers, even when it shows pre-approved, the little asterisk will refer to a very hard to find spot that reads something like: "Subject to a credit bureau report and meeting income requirements." It also notes that you may not actually qualify at all, or they can substitute a different card. If that happens, do not activate the card until you check all the details, rates and fees as they may be very different than the card you had applied for. So getting a pre-selected application should only create as much excitement as that Publishers Clearing House letter stating *you may have already won.*

Killing Your Credit Card

Terminating a credit card is more than just putting it away, but that should definitely be the first step. The card is still perfectly valid and continues to stay active and alive. Obviously, the issuer will send out mailings to entice the holder to start using it again, as they want their card getting lots of exercise.

To ensure a credit card is properly closed, the issuer must be notified. This can be done whether the card is paid in full or not. It is a simple matter of cutting the card in half. The next step is to mail a note asking for the account to be closed and the credit bureaus advised.

Chapter 4

Furniture, Fridges and Other Loans

Consumer and personal loans come in all shapes, sizes and types. When money isn't borrowed on a line of credit or for a mortgage or vehicle (which are discussed in their own chapters), it's generally for consumer products. Personal loans aside, it is also the area where fees, gimmicks and promotions play a big part in convincing customers to just *sign here* and have it today. What could be more convenient than finding the perfect stereo and a salesperson that can get a credit application processed in less time than it takes to drive home and get the checkbook? Unfortunately, convenience hardly ever goes hand in hand with the best terms. That makes it important to understand what credit offers really mean – and cost. But to start, some insight is needed into what goes on when lenders first see your application.

What happens behind the scenes after you apply for a loan is not really a mystery. Quite simply, the lender is checking out the odds of getting their money back if they say yes. The more money you want to borrow, the longer it will take, the more information you have to give them, and the more questions you will have to answer. It really is that simple. A credit card application comes to a lender with thousands of others each day. It may be a short application for a limited amount of money, which must be processed very quickly because of the volume. On the other extreme, applying for a mortgage includes a large number of steps. Sorry – nobody will lend you tens of thousands of dollars without a whole lot of questions, copies of your tax returns and other steps.

Lenders do want to work with you to make an application into a loan. After all, they all have targets and goals to reach. Plus, they have deadlines and other clients, so during the appointment stick to the subject and answer questions without window dressing or getting sidetracked. Supply factual information and bring along the backup you know they will need. Any delays are not their fault while you're hunting for paperwork. Lenders will not phone around for you, take your word on things, or be able to leave sections of their loan application blank – so be ready, do your homework and show up prepared and focused.

Be truthful and practice full disclosure with your loan officer. They will find out whatever you are trying to hide, anyway. You may as well avoid the embarrassment and get them on your side and wanting to work with you from the beginning. Like people everywhere, lenders will become very leery of helping you after you've spent the first part of the appointment bluffing, evading or exaggerating your income. On the other hand however, that does not involve having to settle for partial answers, not having your questions explained thoroughly or being talked down to. After all, you are the consumer and you're the one who will ultimately be making them a handsome profit with the interest you will pay. You do have to do some negotiating as well. Lenders want to make a certain overall yield (profit) for their company. That does not mean they have to make it all from you, but they will start at their retail rates. In a perfect banking world, everyone pays this rate. But like the automotive business, how many people pay sticker price?

Every application for credit requires a signature or your consent. It allows lenders to check you out, run your credit bureau report, and enter your application into their system. The text above the signature is generally similar to: "I, the undersigned represent that the information in this application is accurate and complete. I am hereby authorizing you to obtain, verify and exchange credit and other information, including credit bureau reports from and with other persons with whom I have, or propose to have financial dealings, or where permitted by law." What this means is:

- You're signing to the accuracy and completeness of the application.

- You're agreeing that they can go ahead and do their credit checks with whomever they choose to contact. Consumer report means your credit bureau; employment verification is infrequently done, and the days of an actual call to your bank are long gone.

- You are giving the OK that they can keep exchanging information with other companies now and in the future.

When this is an application for a credit card, there will also be a notification that you are consenting that your agreement is considered to be executed in the State of their offices. As discussed in the chapter on credit cards, it means the consumer laws of that State govern the agreement, no matter where you actually live.

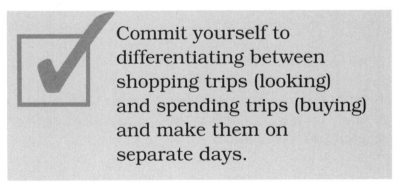

Commit yourself to differentiating between shopping trips (looking) and spending trips (buying) and make them on separate days.

For many personal loans, you will also need to decide whether you wish to have interest charged on a fixed or floating rate basis. Both have their drawbacks and advantages.

Fixed rates have one consistent interest rate for the entire term of the borrowing. Floating rates, also known as adjustable-rate or variable-rate, will have an interest rate that changes during the term. This change is covered by the loan agreement and is generally triggered at specific times. The amount of the change in interest is almost always in relation to the bank prime rate, or other base rate. That is the reason interest is often expressed in terms such as prime plus three. Because the rate will change with market conditions, it will generally be slightly lower. When rates are trending down, floating rate loans are a great idea, but in an environment where rates are moving upwards, it can become a scary and expensive situation.

Can You Afford It?

If your income before taxes is $2,000 and you already have $1,000 in bills – sorry – you're not getting a loan of any kind, at any rate, from anyone, no matter how great the reason. The math says you can't pay it back and why would someone lend you money when they know that you can't afford to make the payments in the future? All lending goes back to something called your debt ratio. It is called your DSR, which is debt service ratio, or TDSR - total debt service ratio.

Your best intentions, excellent credit history or down payment will not make up for the fact that you do not have sufficient income on paper to qualify for the loan. There needs to be sufficient *room* in your gross pay to cover your current bills plus the new payment you are applying for. Calculation sheets for this are at the end of the book, and it is something you can easily do before ever considering a loan application.

Your total debt load ceiling generally cannot exceed 36 percent of gross income before tax. Some lenders use 38 percent while a few will allow a slightly higher ratio. It is a simple matter of taking your monthly pay, times 0.36, to get the maximum amount a lender will allow toward all your payments. When your pay period is not the fifteenth and thirtieth, you will need to calculate your monthly income first:

• Every week – take the weekly pay times 52 divided by 12

• Every two weeks – take the bi-weekly pay x 26 divided by 12

If your pay includes bonuses or commissions that may not be on every pay period, it is best to take your total income over a six-month period and divide it to get an accurate average. From this 36 percent maximum debt, you will need to subtract all your current payments. The chart for this is also at the end of the book. The expenses will include rent or mortgage, only the minimum payments on your credit cards (extra is great but not required), your current vehicle payments, personal loans and anything else. For example:

Gross income per month		$2,777
36% for debt load		$1,000
Current bills	Rent	$ 350
	Credit card payment	$ 45
	Furniture loan	$ 80
Total current bills		$ 475

$1,000 is the maximum debt load you are allowed, and with $475 now owing in payments, it leaves $525 available for new borrowing. On the other end of the scale, if your current bills are already over $1,000, there is no chance of a further loan until some of these payments are out of the way. This calculation is one of the first things your lender will do, so instead of being caught by surprise, it is easier to figure it out in advance.

With $1,000 available toward bills, there are a number of possibilities. There is $475 in bills already, so if the new loan has that amount for a payment, or less, you are within your maximum debt-load and the application can go ahead. Should the new loan have a $580 payment, you will not be approved, as this will push you over the maximum. But you could:

• Pay off your furniture loan, which would add $80 to your payment room.

• Use a down payment for your new loan to get the payments from $580 down to $525 or less.

• Add a cosigner whose income could make this possible (and only if that person has room on their debt load).

What's Your Net Worth?

Lenders all like to know what you're worth in total. Their question is, if everything goes badly, are the odds still good that they will get paid back? Is there enough money or assets to pay off all bills if everything were sold? On some applications, these questions are very limited. For larger loans or mortgages there will be more questions, which relate to your overall financial picture. In the back of the book is a calculation of your total assets – the things you own, and your total liabilities – the things you owe. It is a simple financial statement on yourself and gives lenders the big picture of what you're worth.

Even on simplified credit card applications, there will be a question asking if you are a homeowner or a renter. It tells them a number of things ranging from whether you have some equity (net value) in your home, to the mortgage payments that they use to calculate your debt-load. Often, even short-form applications ask for the house value and the mortgage amount for that same reason. Once again, the more you're borrowing, the more important this information becomes to a lender.

Collateral

All credit is extended on a secured or unsecured basis, which means it is with or without collateral for the loan. In the event collateral is given, the lender will hold a lien against the item until the loan is paid. Should you default on the payments, they will be able to seize or repossess the collateral you put up as guarantee for the loan. This may or may not be enough to clear the balance if the payments are no longer made. It does however, give the lender a larger range of options and a backup plan, should any default occur.

Generally, the larger the loan, the more likely it is the lender requires some security. A mortgage always has the house for security, while loans for a vehicle, RV or boat will almost always require the item being purchased for security.

Any loan without security is called a note, or signature loan. Unsecured credit is found with credit cards, overdrafts and many lines of credit. The better someone's credit rating, the stability at their job and residence, the less likely it is that amounts under five or ten thousand dollars will require collateral.

When They Say No

When you're declined for a loan, the first thing to do is always to ask "Why?" Do not to storm out, get mad or defensive. You can't change or fix anything until you have some answers.

Were you declined because of insufficient income or total debt load? Well, both of these are areas where it is possible, and not that difficult, to make changes. Are you applying for a loan that exceeds what you have for collateral – perhaps a lower amount will work? Would a cosigner be available to sign with you – could that be an acceptable alternative? It is always best to explore all your options instead of going from place to place expecting something different, as their decision will likely be the same. Perhaps you were declined because of a lack of stability. Any frequent change of jobs is always a red flag. Yes, each position may be a better job but their computers don't look at it that way and have no sympathy for the reasoning. Again, it is important to ask the right questions. In this case, how long will I need to be at my present employer to be reconsidered?

It could also be a result of previous credit problems. Lenders are not permitted to give you the specifics from your credit bureau report, but are only able to confirm that you were declined based on information in your file. In fact, the Equal Credit Opportunity Act requires lenders to send you a written rejection letter that outlines the reason for the turndown and also the name of the credit bureau that supplied some of their information. Then you will need to get to work to find out the problem and verify the accuracy. Most people already know – just don't make the mistake of thinking every lender doesn't have access to that same information. You will not find any lender who skips the step of checking it. If bad credit is the issue, you will not talk them out of their decision. There are very few people with enough written documentation and backup proof to turn a declined loan into an approval – and only then with a significant down payment and much higher rate. But as you'll read in the chapter on credit bureaus, there are steps you can take to change your credit score and begin to heal your credit rating.

If You Can't Bank on the Banks

Make your local credit union one of your stops when shopping for your financial needs. They are not-for-profit financial cooperatives whose sole purpose is to meet the needs of their members. This means you actually have a voice and a vote in their operation. With about ten thousand credit unions in all 50 States, almost a third of the population already deals with them, and is familiar with their service, attitude and extensive community involvement. Credit union rates and products are always competitive with other financial institutions, and often better. But where they excel head and shoulders above others is in their member service. Yes, you will be a member-owner and not just a customer. It might not sound like much, but you will quickly notice the difference.

Credit unions can have different membership requirements. These are generally based on common employee groups such as teachers or fire fighters, associations, school or alumni groups, or even entire residential communities. You will also be doing business with someone that is focused on you and your local community. Plus at the end of the year, you will actually receive a dividend (rebate) back on your connection with a credit union. When was the last time your bank actually paid you? A full contact list for your State is in the reference section of the book.

Buy Now - Pay Later

To attract new business, many merchants frequently offer special financing terms. The most common are 90 day no payment offers, no interest for any number of months or even a no payment, no interest, no down payment program. All of these are still loans, they just have some twists designed to entice you to purchase now and avoid the pain of payments or interest – for a while. Even if payments, interest or both can be delayed, they still need to be paid eventually. But will that $1,000 sofa need to be replaced before it is paid off? At the very least, it will no longer look like it did in the showroom a year earlier.

Careful thought should be given to whether delaying the inevitable start is really worth it. Frequently, consumers pretend or really believe that the debt is not real until the due date. The merchant certainly counts on that feeling when they market the program, but nothing could be further from the truth.

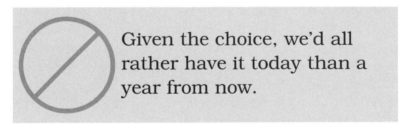

Given the choice, we'd all rather have it today than a year from now.

Merchants sell their finance contracts to outside lenders, mostly finance companies, for immediate cash. These arrangements allow the retailer to be paid immediately when the financial institution buys the loan and actually collects the payments from the consumer later. This will always be disclosed on the application, when it states just above the signature, the name of the actual lender. Merchants do charge a fee for almost all of these offers in the form of an administration, documentation, processing, deferral, handling, or otherwise known fee. The fees are all the same, just called by different names and can range from $29 to over $200. This charge is a profit for the merchant and used toward the costs of these offers. Since these types of financing promotions are hugely popular, we will have a look at each of them separately.

No Interest Promotions

This is a promotion that usually means an interest-free period for six or sometimes 12 months. It is a loan with monthly payments, but without interest charges. If the loan is paid off during the term, it may be a fairly attractive proposition, but will involve paying a deferral or administration fee. Perhaps that still makes it worthwhile, or maybe the promotion is no longer that attractive.

To calculate your total price and payment, you will need to read the fine print of the advertisement or contact the merchant. What you need to know is the amount of the deferral charge and whether taxes and fees have to be paid up front, which is generally the case. On a $1,000 purchase for 12 months without interest (using a seven-percent sales tax in all examples), the breakdown would be:

Price	$1,000
Deferral fee	$ 60
Sales tax of 7%	$ 74
Total amount	$1,134
Down payment (if any)	($ 134)
Balance financed	$1,000

You are financing $1,000 and your payments will be $1,000 divided by 12 for $83 per month since there is no interest to add. You will also pay an additional charge of $60 for their fee. If you take the fee divided by the amount financed times 100, you will see the actual cost of this loan: 60/1,000 x 100 equals an actual interest rate of six percent. Whether it is called a fee or interest, you are paying more than just the cost of the purchase. Plus you may be paying taxes on this fee.

 It doesn't matter if it is called a fee or interest – it's still costing you money.

There is no such thing as free money. The merchant just absorbs the cost of interest. Sometimes the deferral fee covers it all, sometimes retailers cover the additional expense to get your business, or it is built into the price you are paying. When the contract is sold to the finance company, they will deduct the interest from the amount paid to the retailer. It will not be the full rate, but perhaps half the amount (wholesale to merchant) rate.

Remember: The fine print on the contract will tell you that if the balance is not paid in full by the date due, interest is charged right back to the first day of purchase. You snooze, you lose – that $1,000 interest-free will turn into owing $280 or more of interest one day after the due-date.

No Down Payment

Another component in these programs is often no down payment. This is the most perplexing element to understand for credit professionals. Every no down payment sale is always done OAC in the fine print, which is short for on approved credit. In most of these promotions, it also involves paying the applicable taxes up front. Perhaps a little misleading, but the amount they are willing to finance is only the purchase price, not the taxes. All financing without money up front will either increase the monthly payment or lengthen the time it takes to repay. For large ticket items, financing $10,000 instead of $8,000 at six percent, and skipping a $2,000 down payment means the:

• Payment goes up by $61 for three years or $47 for four years.

• Interest increases by $186 over three years or $254 over four years.

It's the old saying: you can pay it now – or pay it later – but later will always cost more.

No Payments – For a While

Another frequently used offer is to promote a no payment plan. This is often used for larger ticket items where it can be of great appeal to many consumers. Obviously, payments will eventually need to be made and over a longer term because of the loan size. Is it an invaluable way to purchase something now and pay later, or just the illusion of getting it today and for free – for a while?

For merchants, it is an attractive advertising campaign used in the fall to defer the payments past Christmas. A 90-day deferral means that the first payment is not due for three months. The interest for this time period is almost always included in the financed amount. Examples of this are detailed in the chapter on vehicle purchases, but are just as relevant for other consumer items.

Careful With Those Credit Offers

All retailers are in the business of selling their products. They're good at what they do and operate in a competitive environment. Offering financing is another way to serve the needs and wants of their customers. Over the past number of years, ads based on payments have become much more common. The largest reason is the consumer's focus on monthly payments instead of the total price. It has also resulted in sales staff often being the middlemen for lenders. Retailers are not in the business of financing their products. They don't have millions of dollars to tie up in a credit department, nor do they want to hire dozens of staff to process applications, or an equal number of collectors. Even huge firms like Sears have sold their credit operations to companies who specialize in this field.

 It's our continued optimism that next year will be better and we'll make more money to pay our growing debts.

Retailers do want to make it convenient for consumers to buy stuff. To accomplish this, they have set up arrangements with lenders to enable the sales staff to take credit applications, fax them to the lender and sign the paperwork right at the store. Each company makes their own decision of which lender they wish to work with. There are a number of ways to pay for a purchase and any one of these is fine with the merchant:

- paying cash
- arranging your own loan
- increasing your overdraft
- setting up a line of credit
- purchasing on a credit card
- taking advantage of the merchant's credit offer

Here are a couple of examples of financing options and offers available through various national companies:

A large computer retailer assigns their contracts to a well-known finance company. Their disclosure is simplified and easy to read, even if it omits some important information. Taking advantage of their financing also attracts an undisclosed administration charge ($99 for six months and $198 for 12 months when you call them) and some ads have shown a *don't pay for 12 months* promotion. There is no mention of zero percent interest, which means you don't make the payments for a year, but the interest meter is running.

The actual finance contract discloses a rate of 23.9 percent. Their normal finance payment requirement is 1/36th of the unpaid balance, which is 2.78 percent per month. This is only $36 the first month (on the example below using $1,282 financed), a payment that keeps getting smaller and can take almost 19 years before the computer is paid off. Do you know many people happy with a 19-year old computer? Isn't that something to consider before paying minimum payments each month? Don't blame the merchant – nobody says a consumer has to choose those terms, or that length of financing.

Don't pay for 12 months just makes this example even worse when considering the total amount paid back:

On a fictitious $1,000 computer:

Price	$1,000
Administration fee	$ 198
Sales tax of 7%	$ 84
Total financed:	$1,282
Total balance after one year:	$1,588

After one year of no payments, the balance is now $306 higher than the start. After all, the interest has been running, but nothing has been paid yet. If the minimum payments now begin, it will be another $3,431 and two decades to pay it off.

However, it takes very little extra to pay it off in only three years. Start by avoiding the one year no payments and get going with putting money toward the balance right away. This will actually match the life of the payments to the (possible) life of the computer. It only means $50 payments, interest of $525, and a total paid of $1,800 (36 months x $50). While this is a realistic plan, it still doesn't make a 23.9 percent rate attractive, and there are lots of financing options far less expensive than dealing with a finance company.

Frequently, a large department store also advertises various finance options with either the *do not pay for one year,* or *12 equal payments – interest-free.* In both cases, a $45 deferral fee applies, the applicable rate is 21.9 percent and the purchase must be on their credit card. After all, what kind of marketing would it be if they didn't leave you with their card in your wallet to use over and over again? An example of a $700 furniture purchase offers a number of choices:

 Not reading or understanding the fine print of ads can be very expensive.

	Pay cash	12 months no interest	Don't pay for 1 year
Price	$700	$700	$700
Deferral fee	N/A	$ 45	$ 45
Sales tax (7%)	$ 49	$ 52	$ 52
Down payment	N/A	($ 97)	($ 97)
Amount financed	nil	$700	$700
Payment/month	N/A	$ 58	0 for 1 year
Interest paid	N/A	none	$153
Total paid	**$749**	**$793**	**$950+**

But in the *don't pay for one year* option, you have not paid for the furniture. You've just avoided the issue for 12 months. The $700 financed and $153 of interest for the year is now on your account and will require regular payments. If you take year two to pay it off, you will have added another $104 of interest, or over two extra years – $207 more. When all is said and done, the original $700 purchase will cost at least 50 percent more.

The Fine Print of Advertisements

The following is an example (yes, it is simplified here) of the text that you need to read carefully to understand the specific terms, fees and rates.

> "Monthly interest is billed but will be waived if minimum monthly payments are made and the balance of the purchase is paid off by the end of the no interest period. Administration fee of $44.95 for 12 month contracts, when blended with interest will effect the annual percentage rate (APR). Example on 12 months no interest option: if minimum monthly payments totaling $611.14 on a $1500 purchase are made and the balance is paid off within 12 months, interest is waived. Then the $44.95 administration fee creates an APR of 3 percent with total cost of $1544.95 on $1500 purchase. If you elect to finance for an additional 12 months, minimum monthly payments totaling $179.36 on a $1500 purchase are made and the remaining balance of $910.34 is paid off at the end of 24 months, interest charges calculated from the date of purchase plus administration fee are $634.65 (total cost $2134.65) and APR is 26.91percent for a $1500 purchase."

Simple right? You only need to imagine this disclosure in an ad roughly the same size print to fit on a postage stamp. What it actually means is:

- The purchase price is $1,500 with a $44.95 administration charge. If $611 in monthly payments is made for a year and the final balance is cleared, there is no interest to pay. Total payback: The $1,500 purchase and $44.95 fee.

- Interest will be billed each month, but waived (not charged). They will bill it, but you won't have to pay it if you come through with a payment before the due date. Late one day or more, and interest at 26.91 percent is charged.

- To extend the contract beyond the 12 months attracts the same 26.91 percent rate, back to day one of the purchase. Take one day longer and you've lost the whole year of interest-free.

- A term of 24 months at minimum payments still leaves a balance of $910. At this point, there will be $590 interest plus the $44.95 administration charge. If the $910 can then be found to pay this in full, the total amount would be $2,135. If not, the meter keeps running for a third year.

You need to make absolutely sure that:

- The balance owing can be paid in full the day it is due or interest starts at over 26 percent. And that the amount does not come from borrowed money or it will just add interest charges somewhere else.

- Pay the $1,500 plus $44.95 over 12 equal payments of $129 (i.e. ignore the minimum payment) and be done with the contract at the end of the year. Spread the whole cost in your budget over a year or be ready for the pain of owing the balance and tons of interest.

- You decide if it is not wiser paying cash or making other arrangements. This skips the delay of paying, as well as the chance of ever being a day late with interest this high, and avoids the risk of this type of financing entirely.

Are Lower Rates Really Cheaper?

If it is only a question of rate, the answer is always yes. Unfortunately with fees and other charges, the answer is not as simple as it seems. Which of these is better on a $2,000 loan for two years - nine percent with no fees, or six percent with a $95 fee? You can't just go by the rate alone and you always have to calculate the total you're paying back to find the answer. Looking up both from the loan charts in the back of the book shows:

$2,000 @ 9% = $91/month x 24 = $2,184 total paid
$2,000 @ 6% = $89/month x 24 = $2,136 + $95 fee = $2,231
(if the fee is financed as well, the interest is even higher)

It is important to discover that only comparing the interest rate is not a solution. You always need to look at the big picture, fees, charges and the TOTAL you are paying when it's all said and done. This includes anything you are paying for up front and all financing costs to get the actual total amount out of pocket.

Borrowing from Friends or Relatives

This is something beyond borrowing five dollars to go to the store because you forgot your wallet. For any larger amounts, if they don't lend you the money – you resent them. If they do – they resent you. Of course, if you don't pay promptly, you will likely avoid them as much as possible and don't really want to face them when you're not paying them back. They will also start judging how you're spending your money. Make it one of your last resorts and strictly a business deal.

• Put it in writing spelling out the amount, interest if any, and a specific repayment schedule. Calculate the interest or a flat amount any way you agree, just make sure it is part of the payments. Why would your relatives or friends be any different than the bank? They won't lend you any money without something in writing either.

- Be honest in asking for what you need and how much.

- Be reasonable and real with yourself when deciding your repayments. Don't promise something you have no chance of meeting and figure out what you can pay. Just because there is no loan officer, it does not take the onus off you.

- Stick to your word – make the payments no matter what. Honor them by paying on time, as they trusted you with the loan when (perhaps) others turned you down.

Don't Forget!

- There is no such thing as a stupid question – it's YOUR money. If you're uninformed or make assumptions, it'll cost you.

- When in doubt – get it in writing in a way that makes sense to you. Don't just let lenders point to a clause in the contract that even a law professor would have to think about.

- Get the fees, additional charges and totals fully outlined.

- Merchants disclose what they are (hopefully) required to – on their terms – in their language – in their best light. Stop them when they use jargon or when you have questions.

- Salespeople are not credit managers. They may have good product knowledge, but they won't give you financial advice. Knowing the questions to ask and getting the right answers is entirely up to you.

- At the end of the day, it is YOU that makes the loan payments, so take the time to think it through and ask questions before signing.

 If your banker sounds like a salesman, professor or politician, consider going somewhere else.

Chapter 5

Automobile Loans

Be careful reading this whole chapter at once, as you will likely just get a headache. To paraphrase consumer advocate Phil Edmonston: There's the truth, there's fiction and then there's automobile-speak.

 There is no such thing as too much information and homework when it comes to automobile shopping.

Long gone are the days when everyone could afford to trade in a vehicle every two or three years. Pressure on the manufacturers has vastly improved the quality of all vehicles. This makes it possible for consumers to keep them for a longer period of time - either by necessity or choice. They are also more expensive, with an average sticker price now over $30,000. No wonder seven out of ten people finance their vehicle purchase and it is their biggest expenditure next to buying a home. Plus, anyone trying to save enough to pay cash sees that the goal posts keep moving. Average new vehicle prices have increased at far greater rates than inflation. It is not because car manufacturers are greedy or less productive than other businesses. A large part of their costs are the ever-evolving technological advances that most consumers demand.

The sections in this chapter are broken down into the most common areas of financing, as well as the various options, rebates, rates, and other choices. The same information also applies to boats, snowmobiles and recreational vehicles. Their purchases may not be as common, but these industries operate very much like the automotive business.

From the original times of financing the first Model T cars, the area of automobile, boat and RV financing has come a long way. When anyone spends this much money, a lot of research, consideration and thought goes into the purchase. Unfortunately, how to pay for it often becomes an afterthought. But just like shopping for a house and mortgage, this is an area that is even more important than finding the vehicle itself.

When you have found your vehicle and agreed to the price, the sales person will always send you to the dealership finance department first. Their job is to take a deposit from you and to get your financing business. If you can trust yourself not to sign anything on the spot, you may get a head start of exploring your options. It is the responsibility of the finance office to ensure the financing happens and terms are acceptable to the purchaser. Make no mistake, it is a large profit center, and the business manager is entirely on commission and understands the sales game much more than the financial field.

Don't worry, there is no need for a financing course. You just need to understand that there are three main factors influencing any loan. These are the interest rate, the term and the total amount borrowed. And then there are the gimmicks, free trip and limited time offers. All of them ending with that famous phrase: *see dealer for details.*

The ideal financing for your vehicle should be set up within your budget and on your terms, with the main goal of making the payments end as fast as you can afford. It should be a fixed payment schedule where there is a definite end in sight. Plus it should NEVER have you owing more on the vehicle than it is worth and the financing should NEVER be longer than its useful life. Yet unfortunately this happens thousands of times a day with painful and expensive consequences. Often, it means just being honest in realizing you cannot afford the vehicle you really have your heart set on.

Some of the most dangerous situations that can create problems, extra expenses and little hope of trading in the vehicle for a number of years are:

- small or no down payments and/or financing the sales tax
- simply taking the longest term available
- vehicle shopping on payments alone
- buying a vehicle beyond a set budget of price or payments
- taking advantage of special offers without realizing the total cost or implication
- longer term financing on a used vehicles which is beyond its reasonable life-expectancy
- signing a lease or balloon contract without understanding the mileage penalties, tax, or wear and tear costs
- not comparing the choice of rebates versus rate breaks in their total payback
- trading after two or three years while financing for five or six
- *pretending* to pay cash by adding a vehicle onto a mortgage or line of credit hoping to achieve lower payments

This last point deserves a special mention as it happens quite frequently. Consumers are re-mortgaging, or adding a second mortgage, to pay cash for their vehicle purchase as they see it. Nothing could be further from the truth. If this new mortgage is amortized over five or six years, it may very well make sense. Unfortunately that is hardly ever the case. Mortgages are set up for very long terms and now include money to pay for the vehicle. Yes, the interest costs may be tax deductible, but at what overall cost? It still creates the dual challenges of having payments hidden in the mortgage for much longer than the life (or ownership) of the vehicle and potentially costing significantly more in interest, while risking the house for the sake of a vehicle should something go wrong.

 A fifteen or thirty-year mortgage for a five- or seven-year vehicle life is never a good idea.

Adding a $25,000 vehicle to a mortgage does reduce the payments, but could cost a lot more interest, and may be stretched out over a much longer period of time.

Financed	Term	Payment	Total interest paid
Car loan	4 year	$604	$ 4,015
at 7.5%	5 year	$501	$ 5,057
Mortgage	10 year	$271	$ 7,558
at 5.5%	15 year	$204	$11,769

Let's face it, financing their vehicle is the only choice for most people. On the surface, who wants to spend $25,000 when you can spend only a few hundred dollars for the same vehicle (per month)? That is the main force behind advertisements, which are now geared more toward promoting payments instead of the price. When financing a vehicle you will need to make a decision before ever leaving the house. Do I just want to worry about the monthly payment today, or the big picture of the total financing and interest costs? It will matter a lot in the future.

Buy New or Used?

Ah, there is nothing quite like that new car smell is there? It has never been driven, no dings, has all the latest options, full warranty and your choice of color. Then there are the manufacturers who offer a rebate or subsidized interest rate almost year round to earn your business. Let's face it, the manufacturers have no vested interest in selling a used vehicle. It has been sold once already and they've made their money – only new vehicles keep the factory running and pay their bills. Yes, dealers sell used vehicles, but rebates and great rates will always be restricted to marketing brand new models.

For all the positives, when you purchase a new vehicle, it is important to understand that you are not buying an asset. Your vehicle will not be worth more next month than it is on the dealer's lot. How much will it depreciate? It's different for every model, but a rough guide is often 20 percent or more in the first year. An easy way to find out is to check the price of a comparable one-year old model. It takes only a couple of minutes to flip through ads, check some Web sites, or the dealer's used car lot to at least get the retail resale value.

Then there is the issue of taxes. The more you pay, the higher your taxes will be since they are based on the purchase price. With a trade, the tax, in most States, will be on the difference you are paying. But still, paying more for the vehicle also means paying more tax.

When purchasing a used vehicle, it will definitely take a little more work. You also have to be flexible and a little sharper when it comes to the price. After all, no two are exactly alike, which makes comparison shopping more challenging. One has low mileage, the other has more features, one has new tires while another, and so on.

 The average vehicle lifespan is 12 years or 126,000 miles, while the average person trades or sells it in 4.5 years and 41,000 miles.

Source: U.S. Department of Transportation

You also will not get a cool rate or rebate, but you will definitely pay less than the price of a new one. On used vehicles, promotions such as rebates, trips or toasters are covered by the seller and are built into the price. It might still be a good deal, but anything added to the cost will naturally drive up the price since there is no such thing as free anything. It is also unlikely that the seller will just absorb the cost of these gimmicks since they also have to make a profit on the deal.

No matter what vehicle, you will first need to negotiate the price. The few exceptions are dealers which have a one-price system. But be sure that is really the case.

If you have decided on a new vehicle, you will need a bit of a road map to guide your way through the minefield of offers. The vast majority of problems occur when customers arrive at the dealership expecting one thing and finding out something quite different. For most, shopping starts with a look through the newspaper ads or some offer on the radio. Manufacturers advertise as well – quite a bit in fact. But their ads are generally targeted to a national audience and promote specific models, their features and values, and their ads will have the best disclosure information. But the real competition for your business is on the ground between dealers.

Take the Rebate or Cool Rate?

One of the first decisions to make when you've found your new vehicle, is whether you want the factory subsidized rate or cash rebate. These are always offered as an either-or. Great rates target the majority of customers who make their buying decision based on payment terms. For this very budget-sensitive group, a change of $20 or $30 might well send them to the competition in search of a lower payment. In order to keep attracting cash purchasers as well, the manufacturers offer a rebate.

Ads are always quoted after the rebate is deducted since no dealer wants to advertise a higher price than necessary. Every ad promotes the low cash price, even though less than 30 percent of customers pay cash. Yet in that same ad, when you see payments advertised, they use the cool rate instead. Once again, a dealer does not want to voluntarily advertise a higher payment than necessary. All the fine print (hurray for at least some disclosure legislation) shows rebates and rate programs are mutually exclusive. It means you can have one or the other but not both. The ads will also show that the price is *rebate to dealer*. That's their words for having already deducted it to come up with the price. Ok, do you have a headache already? It is not that difficult to understand with an example.

Throughout this chapter we will use a fictitious car as a comparison. Each example uses a seven-percent sales tax for ease of comparison. If your tax is higher, it will only have a small impact on the examples. On the other hand, if you live in a State with lower tax rates, the comparisons are still valid but your totals will just be slightly less.

Our fictitious Coolcar has an advertised price of $20,000 and the fine print shows: with rebate to dealer. What this means is that the price is really $23,000, and then it is your choice of 2.9 percent financing or a $3,000 rebate. What they are saying is that: we have advertised this car using the rebate so we can show the lower prices and get your attention. We know most of you will finance, but we will deal with that when you come in. The full information actually breaks down as follows:

Price	$23,000
Less the rebate	($ 3,000)
Sales tax of 7%	$ 1,400
Total amount you owe for the car paying cash	$21,400

If you are paying cash, that is the amount, unless the dealer charges other fees that you cannot negotiate out, or you purchase anything additional. It is based on your State treating the rebate as a manufacturer's discount. If not, you will be charged the sales tax on the rebate as well.

One of the finance choices is to take the cool 2.9 percent rate from the manufacturer. Down payments are always important, but in these examples they have been omitted.

Price	$23,000
Sales tax of 7%	$ 1,610
Total amount (since there won't be a rebate)	$24,610

At 2.9 percent over 48 months, your payments will be $544 per month and you are paying back a total of $26,112 (48 x $544). A total of only $1,470 interest, but then you gave up the rebate to get this cool rate offer.

What almost all customers miss is that there is another option. What if you would like to use the rebate, but still need financing? Using the rebate means you are financing a lot less right from the start, but then you cannot get the advertised rate. Yet you can take a regular rate loan and still keep your cash rebate. A great rate helps a little bit each month, while a lump sum rebate comes off the top immediately to finance a lot less.

The price of the vehicle (like the cash example) is $21,400. At seven percent, the payment is $512 for four years. Hopefully you have already noticed that this is $32 less than using the 2.9 percent rate! The total amount you are paying is $512 x 48 months or $24,576. Yes - $1,536 less, even though your interest rate is higher. Every rebate and rate combination is a different amount and term, so you always have to calculate both options with your specific figures. If you are having flashbacks to your last purchase, this will serve as a reminder that there are always options available if you take the time to ask questions and do some quick calculations.

 **Always add up the full amount of down payment and monthly charges to calculate your real costs.**

Down Payments

The less you finance the better, and the sooner the debt is paid off. When it comes to down payments, more is always better. It will save interest and reduce the monthly payments. Our example has $1,400 in taxes, and without a down payment to at least take care of this amount, it adds $209 in interest and increases the payments by $34 per month over four years just to finance the sales tax. When the sale is made, the dealer remits all taxes to the government, whether the sale was cash (dealer has collected it) or financed (taxes are included in the loan). Yet without a down payment, their hangover becomes part of the payments and debt for the entire life of the loan.

Without paying at least the taxes up front, significant problems can arise later. Should you sell or write off the vehicle in a year, you have paid $408 out of $1,400 in taxes (with the interest). Since they are in each payment over the full term, you still have most of the taxes owing with your loan. After one year, there is still a large amount left on the vehicle and almost another thousand dollars in taxes included in it.

Zero Percent Financing

Finally something that is easy to understand. This is a promotion many manufacturers have run from time to time. It is very expensive because they are subsidizing the entire interest cost, therefore it can often be something close, like a 0.9 percent rate. It is an offer that even cash buyers frequently take advantage of since their savings can stay in the bank and keep making (taxable) interest of some kind. But a zero percent rate certainly isn't for everyone. It requires an above average credit rating and a lot of *room* in your budget to take on this high payment. The better the rate, the shorter they want to lend it to you, so a zero percent rate will almost always be for three years or less, making the offer very attractive, but at a high payment.

To calculate the monthly payments, take only the total financed divided by the term of the loan. For our example it is $24,610 divided by 36 months, which makes the payments $684. The total to pay is the same as the amount financed, since there is no interest to include. There is also no rebate to use since you took advantage of the rate offer instead.

Do Not Pay Until 2015

Ok, maybe not quite that long, but dealerships do advertise no payments for three, four or even six months. Is that good news or a bad idea? From a marketing perspective, it is certainly a very good promotion. It works - so they keep doing it, in many more industries than just automotive. It draws customers that would otherwise not be considering their purchase – at least not yet. But you have to be realistic. If you really need this no payment period what will be different by that time? Will you really have an after-tax raise to make the payments? Not likely. Will another bill be completely paid off so that you can take that amount and use it toward the vehicle payment? Or are you just wanting the vehicle today and delaying the inevitable?

This promotion is called a payment deferral. But it is not a guaranteed offer for everyone. The advertisements always state OAC: On Approved Credit. Deferral terms are given only to those applicants with above average credit and without maximum debt load. Yet it is consumers with lower incomes and larger debts who find this promotion most attractive. For lenders, it's a higher risk since they know that payments will not start for six months and the vehicle is still depreciating. The lender won't be getting money from you, or even hear from you, for some time to come. Yes, many customers love the no payment option and often view this as a temporary free car but nothing could be further from the truth.

The two most important factors to keep in mind are that:

• The interest meter is running – it does not state interest-free. Three, four or six months of interest are still accumulating while you are not paying it - or anything toward principal.

• The value of your vehicle is decreasing during this time while your loan is increasing.

For our used Coolcar, using six months no payments:

Price of vehicle	$24,500
Sales tax of 7%	$ 1,715
Less down payment	($ 3,000)
Total financed	$23,215

On a five-year loan, using a nine-percent rate, you will still have 60 payments; they just won't start for six months. So you really owe the money for five-and-a-half years instead. The payments will be 60 x $500, which blends in (includes) the interest during the six months of no payments. That amounts to $178 a month, or a total of $1,068.

You have financed just over $23,000, but at the end of six months you haven't even started. Yet on that date, your balance is really $1,068 higher and you now owe over $24,000. Six months into making payments - a year from the purchase date - and your balance will still be over $22,000. What you have really done is to put yourself in a situation where you'll owe more than the vehicle is worth for years to come.

What Do You Want For a Payment?

Somewhere along your journey of buying a vehicle almost every sales person will ask you that very harmless sounding question. Almost all people give an answer, and it can cost them a lot of money. What you should be hearing is: *Do you want to just give me a blank check?* The answer to that question is easy, isn't it? Nothing suits dealerships better than to have customers focus on the payment and not negotiating the vehicle price! Let's face it, they would rather haggle over $10 a month, which might add up to $600 for a five-year loan, than to focus on a $1,500 price reduction. Plus the dealer will almost always be able to accommodate your payment.

After all, it doesn't appear to be important that the loan could be over five years (you'd pay about $17,000), six years (you'd pay over $19,000) or even a long term lease or balloon contract, which moves the price you'd be paying even higher. It is by far the best opportunity for dealers to mark up their rate, charge you a price others would never consider or include additional charges and add-ons with little objection. All that and your payment can still be exactly what you wanted. So answering this question is as deadly as seeing only a payment advertised on the window of a vehicle.

Those Other Gimmicks

Many people believe you can tell a lot about the professionalism and credibility of a dealership by their promotions. Whether that is accurate or not, some of the more questionable ads must be working or they wouldn't keep using them. When they involve spending your hard-earned money or financing, they are worth a quick review.

 Just because you're sitting on the other side of the desk doesn't mean you're not in control.

Lenders on Site to Fight for Your Credit Approval

No, sorry. Lenders are at home on the weekends and after 6 p.m. when you're likely to go vehicle shopping. The dealer has the forms from many lenders, so they can take the applications on their behalf. But they are not in the back office with a coffee just waiting to wrestle over your deal and auction off the lowest rate. Besides, it's a competitive environment for them as well. Any small rate change by one quickly has others matching it to keep their share of business.

However, the lenders only give dealerships their base rates and rules of how much they can increase (sell) these rates by. It is the finance manager who sells the rate and picks a lender – mostly the one who lets them bump up the rate the highest. It will range from a base rate (small profit for them – good for you) to a large marked-up rate (profitable for them – very bad idea for you).

Absolute Lowest Payments

Yes, they may be, but the lowest payment is always the absolute longest time financed. This is certainly one of the most dangerous, expensive and useless advertisements. After all, the lowest payment has to be over the longest term possible. So the longer the financing – the higher the total interest cost will be. It takes the focus off the price of the vehicle and is intended to get the sale based only on payments. Once again, it is important to look at the disclosure. A dealer may be using seven-year payments. It could be the lowest, but is that the biggest factor? Knowing the importance of the total paid, wouldn't a $20 higher payment make more sense if it saves thousands of dollars in interest, and takes a year or two off the financing instead?

We Accept all Applications with Guaranteed Approval*

Sad, but true, that up to one-third of the population are unable to qualify for conventional car loans due to credit problems, bankruptcy or many other reasons. The financing hope for this group is called subprime. It comes with huge rates, if there is an approval at all. For a long time, these customers were simply turned away, but in the last ten years they have become a great focus for dealerships, and are many of their most profitable customers. Financing does involve vast amounts of work and challenges for the dealer, with a below average approval rate. Advice to these clients can fill an entire book on its own. Unfortunately, ads for these customers often do very little but encourage consumers falsely. Again, it is the job of the advertisement to get buyers in the door – in this case to give them hope and encouragement.

It is not the dealership's job to talk you out of things— that is totally up to you.

As the tiny asterisk in the heading shows, the fine print will include words to the effect that down payments may be required for guaranteed approval. When interest rates range from zero to 24 percent, where on the credit risk scale would these people be? Certainly not anywhere near the zero percent side of the equation. Yes, every application is accepted – that just means holding their hand out and saying thanks for giving us the credit application – it has nothing to do with being accepted. After all, anyone can have an approval. A worst case scenario is a 95 percent down payment, isn't it? Plus you can be assured that the dealer will mark up their interest rate and often insist (although it is not legal) that the loan must be insured with life and sickness coverage "required by the lender", which is never the case. But then, these subprime clients are often grateful just to be approved, and quite incorrectly don't feel they are in a position to negotiate much of anything.

When used correctly, subprime financing can be an good avenue when no other options exist. Done badly, this type of financing is a huge rip-off for consumers who can least afford it and tend to be less educated about credit in the first place. This is certainly the group toward which aggressive marketing by subprime lenders is directed. Of course, these lenders will approve an application. After all, it is not their job to first explore other alternatives, or to point out someone could have gotten regular rate financing.

For individuals with credit challenges, most dealerships send these applications to the same group of lenders. Anyone who falls into this category needs to understand that applications at more than a few dealers will likely result in the same answer, as the application is ending up at the same lenders. Sadly however, the need for transportation has millions of people making finance payments where the interest paid is actually more than the price of the vehicle. Yet, often just delaying the purchase by six months or a year can improve a credit situation and FICO score (see credit bureau chapter). For anyone with patience, a 10 percent reduction in interest rates is possible and quite likely. On a $15,000 vehicle over four years, that would save almost $4,000 in interest.

Extra Fees and Charges May Apply

Well yes, they will apply and the list can be lengthy. One of the most expensive is often the added charge for delivery. North American Manufacturers include them in the vehicle pricing. Imports often do not – but dealers are mostly free to determine the amount. If they are selling the vehicle in your town, shouldn't they pay to get it there? A few calls on this quote may save you even more than shopping around for the interest rate.

Another charge is the dealership documentation, conveyance or otherwise-known fee. These add up to some of the biggest profits for the dealership and can often be more than the income on a vehicle sale. But again, it is up to the buyer to negotiate a fair total price, which includes the extra fees and charges – or to keep shopping around. Besides, no dealer will lose a sale over the added paperwork fees.

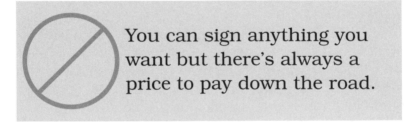

You can sign anything you want but there's always a price to pay down the road.

When Something Has Gone Wrong

Last but not least, all these contracts are covered by something called the doctrine of holder-in-due course. This legal wording simply means the company doing the financing is protected. A lender purchases the contract in good faith and payments have to be made. No matter what dispute the buyer has, from misrepresentation to faulty merchandise, or a host of other problems, the issue is not with the lender. They were not involved and have a right to be repaid. The buyer can certainly pursue the seller through whatever avenues are available, but cannot stop making payments to the lender.

Where to Finance

When the time comes to deal with the financing, there are three main avenues. It should never be an issue of finding the fastest, but rather the one with the best financial terms available. It is most important that you always obtain at least two rate quotes for your financing. This ensures that nobody is ever selling you an interest rate which has been marked up (inflated), is higher than what other lenders offer, or than your credit rating allows.

Lenders get their automotive business directly from customers walking into their branch or indirectly by referral from dealers. Direct lending lets lenders market to their own clients, do their own applications, sell their own products and complete all the loan documents.

Indirect lending is financing through the dealership. Lenders keep control over the credit decision, but do all their processing in one office behind the scenes. In return, they pay dealers a referral fee by letting them mark up (increase) the rate they can charge the customer, or a flat amount of the total loan. Credit applications are faxed to the lender's automotive division and a response comes usually in an hour or less. The contracts are then signed with the dealer outlining the full details of the loan and pledging the vehicle as collateral. After that, the contract is sold to the lender to whom all payments are actually made.

The third source is the finance division of the manufacturer. Some of the better known are General Motors Acceptance (GMAC), Ford Credit and Honda Finance to name a few. All new vehicle low rate financing goes through them, depending on which manufacturer. That means a low rate finance contract on a new Nissan will need to be done through a Nissan dealer and can only be financed with Nissan Motor Acceptance.

In good times or bad, the larger operations like Chrysler Financial or GMAC contribute literally billions of dollars to the bottom line of their parent companies. In fact, GMAC even owns a real estate firm, a mortgage corporation and Ditech, the very aggressive mortgage broker that anyone with a television set has seen advertisements for.

Their mandate is to make a profit, but also to serve dealers. Ford Credit can even approve an application in less than a minute if it falls within certain criteria. The business manager simply enters the application onto a computer screen and presses the send button. On a large percentage, an approval will flash across their screen in an instant. The application is scored; a credit bureau pulled and the figures are reviewed. Yes, it impresses customers, but then the name of the game is to get the customer from purchase decision to delivery in as little time as possible. That is a process you need to slow down and step back from. Shopping around and buying should always be on different days. A small deposit marked 'subject to suitable financing' will always hold the vehicle so you can do your rate shopping and some math to figure out the total you'll be paying back. If the dealer won't hold it with a deposit, that is probably not the place where you'll want to buy anyway.

What is important to remember is that the finance office of a dealership wants to be involved in the loan. Only then are they able to sell after-market products, bump (increase) the interest rate charged and sell life or sickness insurance as part of the loan, lease or balloon contract. As they work for the dealer, it is always wise to get all the figures and information and shop around for the financing, just as much as the purchase.

Balloon Contracts

Balloon contracts have been around for some time, but have only become popular in the last number of years. They may go by different names but they are all the same. Ford calls them Red Carpet Option, while GM's name is SmartBuy, for example. They were a response by various lenders and manufacturers to the option of leasing. Since leases often produce lower monthly payments, this allows the same general benefits, while customers actually have title to the vehicle.

The major difference from leasing is that balloon loans require tax to be included up front in the purchase amount. They are three, four or five year loans with this balloon amount owing at the end. After the completion of the actual finance portion of the contract, the customer is able to return the vehicle. Just like leases, this creates the option of walking away if the amount at the end is higher than the value of the vehicle. Pay only about half, pay only what you use and other similar slogans are some of the marketing phrases used.

Different lenders have different charges, but you will always be liable for any over-mileage penalty beyond the limit of your contract (generally 12 - 15,000 miles per year) and damage above normal wear and tear. Most of them also have a drop-off or disposition charges for the right to walk away. In the event that the balloon balance is worth paying, it will still mean re-financing the amount if you are not able to pay cash when the balance is due. Don't be surprised however, if it turns out that after all those years of payments, the balloon balance is almost the same as the vehicle is worth. The end-value calculation comes from a guide published by the same people who issue the famous used car value guides. These charts just project future values four or five years ahead. They are not designed to help build equity, but only to have payments keep up with the depreciation of the vehicle.

Leasing Made Simple

A lease is an alternate way of paying for a part of your vehicle. It is the automotive equivalent of *pay as you go* cell phones, and in most ways very similar to balloon financing. To reduce the monthly payments, a lease takes the future value of the vehicle out of the amount financed. It allows payment for what you are using and not the entire vehicle. That part left out of the financing for the end is called the residual or buyout. On a three-year lease, the estimate might be that the vehicle is worth 40 percent at the end. On $20,000, that takes $8,000 off and charges principal payments only on the other $12,000. There will still be interest on the whole amount – after all you're driving the whole vehicle, but you are paying back only the $12,000 that you are *using*.

But when the lease is over, the vehicle isn't paid for. The $8,000 that was left out now has to be dealt with. It is your option of what to do, and your choices at the end of the lease are to:

• Walk away from the buyout balance – after all, if it's not worth that much, why would you want to pay it? Dropping off the vehicle does mean you will have nothing to drive and nothing to show for years of payments. You will also pay for any damage, missing equipment and extra mileage since every lease comes with a restricted amount of mileage.

- Sell it or trade it – you still owe $8,000 plus the tax but anything more than that is yours (it is called equity – the difference between what you owe and what it's worth).

- refinance the balance to finish paying it off. A new loan takes the $8,000, adds the tax and finances this for another term.

 If you lease: Longer terms reduce the financial advantage. A lease over three years seldom makes sense.

You negotiate the price on a lease the same way as a purchase and it will affect your payment. The buyout at the end doesn't change – it is always a percentage of the sticker price so it is the same for everyone by region or nation-wide. However, a lease is not like renting a car for a couple of months. You cannot simply return the vehicle before the end of the contract. It is called an early termination and will be very expensive.

Leasing reached its peak in the late 1990s, but has backed off significantly since then. Ford has always been recognized as the leader in leasing with their two-year terms called *The Plan*, or *Red Carpet Lease*. They were the first to recognize that customers can have a reasonable payment for a short term, and dealers were able to have a supply of good, late-model used vehicles when customers traded in their leases just two years later. After all, a $2,000 down payment over 24 months lowers the principal payment by $83. That same amount on a 60-month contract only reduces it by $33 per month. For many customers it always seems better to cut $83 off the payment than $33. It does not address the total payback or anything else, but on the surface seems very appealing.

The tremendous explosion of leasing quickly became a challenge for manufacturers. The biggest problem was the vast number of lease returns where customers owed much more on their buyout than the value of the vehicle. That became expensive and flooded the market, with some manufacturers having tens of thousand of vehicles dropped off in some months. Over the last few years, their attractiveness has been scaled back after manufacturers lost hundreds of millions of dollars on end-value guarantees (residuals) that proved to be too optimistic. Terms have now been extended to keep the vehicle on the road a little longer, while residual (end) values have become more conservative (lower).

Is leasing an attractive alternative to financing? Certainly. Is leasing an advantage over financing? Perhaps. Each vehicle is as different as the needs of a customer. Not every person (hopefully) only considers the payments. It is also an issue of the total payback and, in the case of leasing, other factors as well. One of the more costly ones is the lease acquisition fee, bank fee, lease inception fee or otherwise known charge. This is not something due on a finance contract and is often marked up by the dealership. This can range from a few hundred dollars to over $1,000 for either leases or balloon contracts.

Leasing comes with its own jargon, sometimes for no reason other than to confuse customers. Once again, it pays to ask questions or to walk away. The most confusing can be their use of a money factor. It may be quoted as 0.005 and sure doesn't tell a customer much. It is simply a number more suited to calculating lease payments. But if you do hear a money factor and an evasive answer of what the actual rate is, simply grab the salesperson's calculator and multiply the factor by 2400 to get the rate. In this case, it is 12 percent, and never difficult to calculate on your own.

Back to our Coolcar on either a lease or purchase. A balloon contract works the same way, other than the taxes being part of the financing. This example is based on no down payment and uses a seven-percent sales tax for simplicity, ignoring all other taxes, levies and charges.

	Purchase	Lease
Manufacturer sticker price		$24,700
Price of vehicle	$23,000	$23,000
Tax of 7%	$ 1,610	n/a
Lease fee	n/a	$ 400
Total starting balance	$24,610	$23,400
Rate	7.5%	7.5%
Term	60 months	36 months
Base payment		$ 499
Tax on payment	N/A	$ 35
Total payment	$ 493	$ 534
Buyout balance (37%)	none	$ 9,139
Tax on buyout	N/A	$ 640
Total payback	$29,580	$29,003

Remember:

• A lease fee would not apply to a purchase contract.

• A purchase could have a low-rate finance or rebate offer, which will reduce the payment and the total amount paid.

• You cannot predict the future, so be careful. Walking away from the buyout means needing another vehicle right then, no matter what your credit or employment situation is at the time.

Explaining the lease:

• A lease is paying for a portion of the vehicle and then dealing with the buyout balance at the end of the term.

• Tax on leases is paid with each monthly payment. It will also be charged on the buyout balance if the vehicle is purchased at the end of the term.

• If the customer wishes to keep the leased vehicle at the end, the balance owing will be $9,139 and another $640 in taxes. Or, a new loan will be set up to pay this for another two years ($782 interest) or three years with $1,172 interest.

• You will almost always be charged your first payment and a refundable security deposit that will be held for the term of the lease, similar to renting an apartment.

- There are always mileage restrictions and driving more will cost a lot in penalties. But leases can easily be set up for whatever mileage the customer needs. It just moves the payment up and the buyout (end value) lower.

Some Leasing Advantages:

- You are not financing your taxes up front.

- Down payment has a bigger impact on payments.

- Monthly payments are often lower.

- Terms are almost always (or should be) shorter.

- Someone else has the risk of guessing the future value and the problem of getting rid of it if they guessed wrong (too high).

- No pretending it is an asset to pay off as quickly as possible. It is just an expense each month like cable TV or your gas bill.

- Maybe you can only afford to finance a Focus, but leasing might let you drive a Mustang if you choose.

Some Disadvantages of Leasing:

- The interest charges are for the full amount of the vehicle price, but the principal payments are only on the price less the end-value (the reason for lower payments).

- You are responsible for over mileage and excess wear & tear.

- A few years from now the balance will still be approximately what it is worth – there will not be much equity, if any.

- If you're keeping the vehicle there will be another round of financing the buyout, plus tax.

- Higher depreciation on all vehicles occurs in the first years. It results in larger total payments for a relatively shorter time frame on the road.

- When a lease needs to be broken before the expiry, the costs can be as high as all the outstanding lease payments still left.

Chapter 6

Lines of Credit

Not too many years ago, a properly trained and capable lending officer, often known in the community, and established in the branch, would actually become involved in the application for a loan. They would take a credit application, review the reason for the loan and even offer a little financial advice or insight.

But internal costs to lend small amounts were becoming very costly when compared to their potential interest income. The alternative for many of these smaller loans was to add it on a charge card, or an overdraft, which was often unacceptable because of the high interest rate for both. Lenders certainly wanted to retain their clients, but also wanted to make each account profitable at the lowest possible expense. The most efficient solution for them and their clients became a line of credit that has always been widely used by corporations to finance their ever-changing inventory and accounts receivable.

In some ways, a line of credit is almost like a checking account. It becomes a permanently useable loan, set up for a fixed amount and continuously available and open similar to a credit card, but with much more attractive rates. It allows a customer the freedom to use any or all of it for whatever reason at any time. In fact, lines of credit come with checks and even an ATM card to be able to access them.

The application process is the same as other bank loans; it's just that you won't need to see your banker any more when you want another loan in the future. On the other hand, it can be like a permanent debt. It allows a one-time set up and turns the discipline of payments over to the priorities of the consumer. A $5,000 line of credit can be used for any reason at any time. Just like the limit on a credit card, this approved amount is in place and its use is up to the individual. When the balance is zero, there is no interest. When a part of it is used, interest is charged on that amount actually owing from that day, until it is paid in full. Minimum payment requirements can vary between lenders, but are usually three percent of the balance outstanding for unsecured lines, and interest is charged only on the actual amount owing. The interest rate is set as a percentage above the prime or base rate, so as rates change, the interest charged will fluctuate as well.

Lines of credit are convenient and allow total control over their use. They are also very flexible in their repayment – for better or worse. As long as minimum payments are made, any additional funds go straight to the principal. The consumer has become the loan officer that decides how much to pay and how quickly to pay it off. It is certainly one of the least costly and most convenient forms of credit. Some ads call them financial freedom, and it is for many consumers. But like anything else, it has to be managed well and kept under control.

Once the line of credit is established, the old structure of loan applications, calculating debt ratios and other steps are no longer needed. The poor customer has now been made the loan officer. With no training and limited knowledge, the holder of the credit line might be well on the way to permanent debt between this account and his or her credit cards. While it can be paid off at any time, it does not have any fixed repayment schedule over a term of three or four years like typical loans do. The chance to make small monthly payments and the financial security of having it continuously available is a big advantage – but it can also be a big risk for those same reasons. Lines of credit are established in two different ways.

Unsecured Lines

For smaller amounts and creditworthy customers, lines of credit are the norm. They will often be in the range of $3,000 to $10,000 or more. Their rates usually range from two to five percent above a base rate, depending on the credit worthiness of the customer, and charge payments of around three percent on the outstanding balance. It creates a small principal repayment each month in addition to covering the interest charges.

Unsecured simply means that there is no actual collateral. They may be harder to obtain, but only require an above-average credit rating and sufficient income to service the debt. With slogans such as never get another loan, 24-hour access and be your own credit manager, every lender has them. Different names, but identical in how they are established and function.

Secured Lines

Lenders love having collateral since it reduces their risk if something goes wrong and payments are not made. For many, the collateral is the equity in a house. When the line of credit is secured by a property, the interest rate will generally be at a base rate or slightly above. After all, the lender has very little risk. Because lenders are now fully secured, they have very little interest in helping anyone pay their balance off quickly, so the monthly payments are interest only, without paying anything toward the principal. That is just fine with the lender, if the truth be known. For them, the longer the debt is outstanding, the more interest they earn.

Their set-up does involve some one-time fees similar to those of a mortgage, including points for the full amount. The financial institution will require a formal appraisal of the home to calculate the value and equity. Each lender has different rules of how much equity in a home can be used to secure a line of credit. Some people would rather re-mortgage than to add a line of credit onto their home, while others want to keep their mortgage in place to avoid refinancing, mortgage penalties or other costs. The following example uses a 90 percent loan advance limit. When you know the value of the home the calculation of the maximum amount available is easy:

Actual appraised value of residence	$100,000
Multiply by the maximum advance of 90%	x 0.90
Equals maximum total loan amount	= $ 90,000
Subtract the entire current mortgage balance(s)	- $ 52,000
Equals the maximum amount available for a line of credit	= $ 38,000

The second step is to figure out if your debt load can afford this maximum line of credit, or whether a lower amount needs to be applied for. This is also a simple calculation:

Secured line of credit with interest only payments:

$ _____ x ____% /100 /12 = $ _____
Line of credit   Rate   Minimum monthly
   amount   payment

Unsecured line of credit with a minimum payment percentage:

$ _____ x _____% /100 = $ _____
Line of credit   Minimum   Minimum monthly
   amount   payment %   payment

A line of credit creates long-term debt from short-term bills and spends the equity in your house.

Another major consideration is the interest. Any reference to base rates, prime, or prime plus means that the rate is adjustable. In periods of rising rates this becomes a windfall for lenders who immediately get to pass on the higher interest – but a risk for the borrower. When this happens, few people have the money to immediately pay off the balance to avoid any rate increase. That leaves only two options. One is to absorb the increased interest costs or to re-mortgage (yes, the rates have already increased) to lock in the amount owing before it (potentially) becomes worse. The benefit of a line of credit secured by a principal residence is that at least the interest costs can almost always be tax deductible. This is different than consumer debt and discussed further in the mortgage chapter under home equity lines of credit.

The Risks of Using Them

The biggest drawback of using a line of credit is the discipline required to re-pay the balance. It is well known that only about a third of credit card holders pay off their balances each month. While no specific statistics are released by financial institutions, obviously only a tiny fraction of people actually clear their lines of credit with any frequency.

A line of credit never matches the logical term of a loan. To stress this again, it is easy to fall into the trap of using a line of credit for a longer-term debt than it should be. It is up to every individual to repay the amount in a very disciplined and structured manner. After all, more and more consumers use these credit lines for large ticket purchases such as boats, cars, RVs and even their IRA or 401(k) contributions.

 Make sure to match the length of time you'll take paying it back to the life of the purchase.

A boat that someone plans to keep for four years should properly be financed for four years. This creates equity and saves interest. If a check is written on a credit line there is still financing in place. It is now up to the user to ensure that payments are large enough to pay the balance over an appropriate time. If not, the boat may be quite depreciated, while the balance continues to linger well beyond its useful life. In other words, the boat keeps going down in value while the loan balance isn't moving. Or worse, since there is nobody monitoring the use of the credit line, the boat can simply be sold and the money spent on something else, while the account continues to accumulate interest and eat up monthly payments.

In the example of a $5,000 boat paid through a line of credit at seven percent, you can pay three percent minimum payments each month, which start at $150. But these payments will keep getting less each month. Making minimum payments will take over 12 years to pay and cost $1,165 in total interest. Instead, pay the $150 in fixed installments each month (no matter what the payment says at the bottom of each statement). Now it will take only 38 months and less than half the interest.

Another example is a loan taken for a long-awaited, well-earned vacation. A personal loan would logically be set up over 12 months. The same amount drawn on a line of credit is still a debt, but now nobody is making sure that the balance is paid off before the next vacation. On $1,000 at seven percent, it will actually take seven years to pay with only minimum payments.

Often, when the amount warrants, a personal loan can be obtained at comparable rates. These loans can be both fixed rate and fixed payments. Best of all, they will retire the debt over a fixed period and leaves the line of credit available for emergencies or short-term needs.

Never put yourself into a situation where you owe more on something than it's worth!

Credit lines work best for those who want flexibility or access to the total amount over a longer period of time, drawing funds during a renovation project or other needs where money is required gradually. Interest is then only paid for the amount already drawn (used) and allows the flexibility of repayment terms at the customer's choosing.

Another wise use for credit lines can be for a consolidation. This often includes consolidating credit or store cards, and other bills with higher rates. Consolidating these through a line of credit almost always results in significant interest savings. This is especially true with credit cards that can be up to triple the rates when compared to a line of credit. Consolidations do require an above average credit rating. These can also be a danger sign to lenders as they take a number of smaller loans from different companies, and combine all of them into one account, at the risk of the lender making the consolidation loan.

This is another way that a financial professional or a loan officer can be helpful. While there is an immediate relief in only having one bill now, the amount after consolidation can be quite large. Interest charges may be less, but the total can quickly add up. The point of a consolidation is only achieved if the credit cards are canceled and not run up again, since their amounts are now simply hidden in the credit line debt. A great quote came from Robin Leonard when he wrote: "Sometimes it's a good idea to borrow from Peter to pay Paul - but it depends on who Peter is."

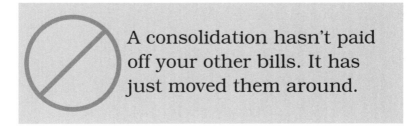

A consolidation hasn't paid off your other bills. It has just moved them around.

No doubt, any line of credit is far preferable to credit card debt or many other consumer loans. But it does take discipline when they are used. When the monthly statement arrives, the only tip a lender gives you is to outline the absolute minimum amount. The rest is up to you. Have you been trained just to pay what they have asked for? Nowhere does it state the time it will take to pay the full balance making minimum payments. For secured lines, it is even possible with interest only to never pay a dime toward the principal. Wouldn't it be a rude awakening if each statement came with a warning: *At your balance of $1,020 with minimum payments, it will take seven years to pay in full?*

Chapter 7

Mortgages

There are really only two ways to buy a house - with your money or with someone else's money. What would baby boomers of the past generations have done without the huge equity they have in their principal residence? This only came about through hard beginnings, a down payment scraped together or borrowed, and a home mortgage.

Over the next year, millions of Americans will deal with a mortgage in one way or another. Many will upgrade to a bigger home or refinance their current mortgage loan. Others will reach their dream of becoming first-time homeowners with the help of a mortgage, which is one of the best ways for anyone to build their wealth.

If It Seems Impossible

Unfortunately, for many lower-income families, this dream can seem impossible. Through the work of many organizations and non-profit groups, there are numerous resources available to help make this a reality. It won't be easy, but it will be possible in direct proportion to how much energy and effort you commit to making it happen. You'll need to commit for a reason – not just a season. After that, you'd be surprised at how many groups and individuals are passionate to teach you about the tools needed to get started. The contact information for America Saves, with groups throughout the country, is in the back of the book. It is managed by the Consumer Federation of America who was also instrumental in the start of the Black America Saves programs. One call and you'll be in touch with many others who share your dreams, goals and desire to look for ways to make home ownership a reality, one step at a time.

One powerful example of this started in early 2004 when Pittsburgh became the first city to launch a Faith Saves

Initiative. This is a program designed to help motivate and educate families on the value of savings and the benefits of home ownership. Under the leadership of Building United of Southwestern Pennsylvania (BUSP), this group has already pulled together over 1,200 churches. Its executive director, Reverend Samuel Ware describes the purpose of BUSP very clearly as "a mission to help people with low to moderate incomes become home owners." The Faith Saves Initiative also has major commitments from Fannie Mae and Countrywide Home Loans. Countrywide is providing $100 million in mortgage loan money to BUSP, and is already a leader in home loans to minorities and lower-income families, along with providing no-cost financial education sessions.

Last, but certainly not least is The Heinz Endowments, whose help was largely responsible for the start of the Pittsburgh program. It is the Foundations' steadfast belief that teaching financial literacy is one of the most important tools for minority and lower income groups to become financially successful and to make the dream of home ownership a reality.

Where there's a will, there is always a way. But you cannot have others fighting harder for you than you are prepared to fight for yourself. If you are someone who believes that owning your own home can't be done, take a look around, and realize that many people are well on their way. So, make a phone call to America Saves, talk to your church leaders, or get a group together and ask a local Credit Union manager to come speak to you. Do whatever it takes, but be the first to make it happen for yourself – not the last one wishing you had.

Shopping for a Mortgage Loan

Obtaining a mortgage loan is almost a dance. Lenders want the largest return with the least risk, while the borrower wants the most generous terms at the lowest rate. This is definitely an area where shopping around for your mortgage can pay off in savings larger than negotiating the actual price of your house. One of the considerations will certainly be the deductibility of mortgage interest. But you can deduct interest on a bad mortgage in the same way you do with a good deal. The IRS allows deduction (with certain rules and limits – so always see a tax expert for your specifics) of interest on the first million dollars of debt on your principal and secondary residences. Plus another $100,000 maximum on second mortgages through lines of credit or other ways. But it should never be the only reason for a larger mortgage loan, or not finding the best deal available.

 **Don't settle! There are tons of mortgage lenders who would love to compete for your business.**

Shopping for a mortgage loan has nothing to do with convenience, and where you currently bank is irrelevant. It's not as if you're ever going to visit your mortgage company for coffee. Whether they are located across town or in a different State, all that matters is their rate, points and terms. The payments will be debited from your account, or mailed, no matter where you live or bank.

Don't be misled by some television ads claiming that the process is either easy or paperless. It is the reason those ads have fine print. Disclosure and the details are very important, but also quite difficult to catch in a 30-second ad. When it comes to taking on a debt of this size, it is not the time to be lazy, complacent, or to only consider the convenience. It will take some work, but it's worth it.

In that same way, no consumer should ever accept the first answer that he or she only qualifies for subprime interest rates. These lenders market extensively to lower-income individuals and minority groups. However, just because someone is told that normal lenders will not approve them does not always make it true. Consumer advocates agree that many subprime loans could have qualified for regular rates if the consumer had only shopped around.

What you are looking for is a pre-approved mortgage. This way, lenders can compete for your business while there is less stress and time constraints. After all, once a purchase offer is in place, there is little time to shop around. A pre-approval is simply a written commitment by the financial institution. This is quite different than simply pre-qualifying which only involves a basic and rough review of your information, debt load and down payment. It's a start, but it is not a commitment at all.

An actual pre-approval, along with a commitment letter, will outline your down payment and set the maximum you qualify for. It will also lock-in your interest rate and points, if you choose, usually for up to six months before the mortgage has to be in place. If rates go up during that time, you are protected and will only pay the guaranteed rate. You can also elect to float the interest rate and lock it in at a later time. Both options come with potential risks or rewards, that only you can decide on.

Lenders look at two different ratios with each application. The first is the total debt service ratio (TDSR or also called back ratio). This is the total of all your bills, including the monthly housing expenses, divided by your monthly pretax income. This usually cannot be higher than 36 percent toward all bills. The second ratio is often called the front ratio and takes your total housing expenses divided by your monthly pretax income. This includes the principal, interest, taxes and insurance and must usually be at 28 percent or less (33 percent for jumbo loans).

While these 28 and 36 ratios are standard underwriting rules they are not written in stone with every lender. For someone with above-average income and credit rating, higher down payment, or other factors, these maximums can certainly be stretched. It is another reason to obtain a pre-approval to know exactly what you qualify for. To calculate your own maximum mortgage payments based on the standard percentages, just complete the income and debt load chart at the back of the book. With these two figures, use an approximate mortgage rate and look up the payments in the back of the book for the term of your choice. For example:

Gross monthly income with your partner	$4,000
28% maximum mortgage payment would be	$1,120
36% of gross income is	$1,440
Deduct total list of current payments	$ 450
Equals total monthly payment available for	$ 990

    mortgage (the lower amount of 28%, or 36% after other bills)

For example, with a rate of seven percent, use the chart at the end of the book to calculate the amount you may qualify for. It will show the maximum amount is just under $150,000, with a payment of $998 for a 30-year mortgage. Add to this the amount of the down payment and you will have the highest purchase price possible. To reduce your debt, or to make your desired payment fit your budget, chapter four outlines some suggestions on lowering your current bills.

In addition to knowing the amount you qualify for and the amount of down payment you've saved, there is more. There are the other costs and surprises you will need to anticipate when purchasing a house, over and above any down payment:

• Application, origination or processing fee – these can range up to $300. Lenders charge this to make sure you're serious but can refund it when you close your mortgage with them.

• Credit report fee – lenders won't do anything without a credit report and can charge upwards of $50 for this.

• Title insurance – this protects the lender and borrower against the possibility that the seller does not have legal title, or future ownership problems. It can range from a few hundred dollars to thousands, depending on the lender and the purchase price.

• Escrow fees – the costs of processing and completing the mortgage loan documentation and advancing the funds. It can vary, but generally is in the range of $300 to $1,000 and depends on the amount of the purchase price.

- Loan origination fee or points – this can at times include the fees for an appraisal, credit report or the escrow fees and is generally referred to as points. While it is possible to negotiate this percentage, it should not come at the cost of a higher interest rate, as reviewed later in this chapter.

- Home appraisal – a lender will always obtain an appraisal to have a written and independent valuation of the property. Their loan amount will be based on this appraisal and you will be paying for it. The law does state that you are entitled to a copy of the appraisal, as you're paying for it.

- Inspection charges – if you are choosing to hire someone to do a full inspection as part of the purchase process, the price will be around $300 to $500.

- Legal fees – yes, lawyers may be involved in completing the mortgage signing and it will be at your expense. In most States it is not a requirement and can be done by a settlement agent when realtors use a standard contract.

- Survey charge – the independent certification that the property and the house meet local laws, easements, size limits, etc. Lenders do not want to find out later that the garage exceeds size restrictions or that the home is built too close to the front of the property.

- Real estate tax adjustment – taxes are billed only once a year. You will be responsible for the adjustment of real estate and school taxes between you and the seller. You will be paying the portion of the year that you own the property.

- Private mortgage insurance – this is required on any mortgage with less than a 20 percent down payment to protect the lender against default when there is a minimal amount of equity as discussed later in this chapter.

- Prepaid loan interest – most lenders require payments on the first of each month. You do need to pay the interest from the day of the mortgage to the first of the following month. You will be safe (and a little high) if you take your mortgage payment divided by 30 days times the number of days left in the month to calculate the amount owing.

- Home insurance – your insurance broker has a software program to calculate the coverage, which must be in place before the loan will be advanced.

- Life or accident & sickness insurance – either are always an optional coverage. Premiums are charged monthly and added to the payment. You can also start coverage after the mortgage is in place and can cancel it at any point. But mortgage life insurance can be expensive and very limiting. It is designed to protect lenders and only pays out the mortgage. While it will leave your family with a paid off home, chances are they may be forced to sell it to raise money in order to make other payments. A term life policy, even for the same amount as the mortgage, is actually payable to your family. It gives them a choice of paying the mortgage or continuing with the payments and having the funds available for other bills. Either way, it creates financial freedom instead of possibly more pain and loss.

 Skip the costly and restrictive mortgage life insurance and consider a term life policy instead.

- Renovations or improvements - that may be required before you can move into the property.

- Other fees and charges – you may also be asked to pay courier fees, notary charges, recording fees or other costs that can add up to another couple of hundred dollars.

- Other costs – especially if you are moving from a rental premise. This can include the typical homeowner starter kit of lawn mower, drapes or furniture, utility transfers, etc.

You can negotiate most fees with the exception of taxes and government filing fees. But it means being aware of them and asking in advance. Often, some of these charges can also be included in the mortgage, instead of being paid up front. While that may sound like a good deal, it simply means there will be interest on them for the next 15 or 30 years. For every $1,000 of fees included in your loan, you will pay around $1,400 of interest over a 30-year term. Reducing out of pocket costs may sound good, but it will still cost you.

 Always know what mortgage fees and charges are paid up front or included in the payments.

The Questions You've Got to Ask

Base interest rates are very competitive between all lenders. But these rates are only benchmarks and don't let you know the fees, points or discounts to negotiate. Just knowing an advertised rate is of very little use. To find the best rate, fees and options, you need to approach lenders with a list of what you want and your questions.

- What are your posted rates or what will you offer me based on my credit rating for charges in points, fees and rates? (Lenders are now required to provide, free of charge, your credit, or FICO score, and factors that have lowered it).

- What is the full list of charges I will be expected to pay?

- If I deal here, will you refund my application fee?

- How long will you need to approve my mortgage, and what is the longest time frame for a pre-approval?

- Do you have bi-monthly payment terms and can I change my payments from monthly to bi-monthly at a later date?

- What are the penalties and pre-payment options?

- I have less than a 20 percent down payment, what are my total mortgage insurance costs or alternatives?

Remember: Getting a verbal answer to some of these questions may make you feel comfortable to proceed, but always get them in writing. You can also have your lender point out specific sections in their loan offer, or other documentation where you'll find answers in words that you understand.

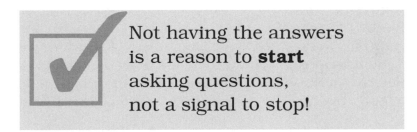

Not having the answers is a reason to **start** asking questions, not a signal to stop!

What Happens When You Apply?

The job of all lenders is to evaluate risk, and for mortgages this involves a lot of questions. Lenders will want all the information on you (or you and your partner). If you already have an offer to purchase a property they will obtain information on it as well. Their first step is to complete a credit application and obtain the backup documents. Requirements vary between lenders, but your homework includes bringing along at least:

• The last two years of W-2 forms.

• The last two years of federal tax returns.

• The two most recent and consecutive pay stubs.

• Proof of other income such as alimony, pensions, social security, disability payments or child support.

• A letter from your employer to confirm employment, income, and whether you are full-time permanent or part time.

• The latest statement for any current mortgage or contact information for your landlord(s) over the past two years.

• A list of assets and liabilities. Complete the schedule in the back of the book and feel free to copy it to take with you, as it will save you a significant number of questions and time. This includes information on any real estate you now own with its value, balance, payment and rental income (if any).

- Three months of statements for your bank account, money market, savings, or certificates of deposit to verify you have the funds for the down payment and closing costs. Lenders need to be sure that this is not from borrowed money.

- Receipts for any loans, credit cards or other bills you have recently paid off as these will not yet show in your credit bureau or your FICO score. It is not necessary to pay off some bills in advance. Your loan officer will review which accounts may not factor into their calculations and which ones are permissible to be paid off to increase the loan amount, or payment maximum you may qualify for.

If you are self-employed, you will need at least two years of K-1s and two years of your partnership or corporate tax returns in addition to your personal returns. Lenders need to verify that the company is making sufficient income, and that you are drawing enough money out of the company to make the payments.

What you will receive within a few days of your application are some documents that you should carefully review for accuracy. These include a Good Faith Estimate of your settlement charges outlining your total costs, fees and charges. You will also get the Federal Truth-in-Lending disclosure with all the details of your loan and a Mortgage Program disclosure from your lender. If you have elected an adjustable rate mortgage, there will also be a booklet entitled Consumer Handbook on Adjustable Rate Mortgages (CHARM).

Make sure you actually receive these documents and copies of what you have signed. According to the Federal Trade Commission, there may be problems ahead if your lender:

- Suggests you enhance or falsify your application.

- Asks you to sign blank forms to 'speed it up' or 'fill it in later'.

- Sells payment terms you cannot realistically meet.

- Attempts to switch the loan arrangement from what you had negotiated and already agreed to.

Common Mortgage Types

Conforming Mortgage Loans

These are mortgage loans that fall within the guidelines and limits of Fannie Mae (Federal National Mortgage Association) and Freddie Mac (Federal Home Loan Mortgage Corporation). In fact, Fannie Mae is the largest source of residential mortgage funds in the country, having funded the loans of more than 55 million households since 1968. Both of these are stockholder-owned corporations which are chartered by Congress and sell their loan portfolios in large blocks to investors. That is the reason for their specific standards and documentation requirements. When a loan exceeds their maximum amounts, it is referred to as a nonconforming, or Jumbo loan. In those cases it will be at a slightly higher rate and can also have some additional requirements.

The actual loan limits change each year. For 2005 the conforming loan limit for first mortgages was just under $360,000 for single-family homes. These limits are 50 percent higher in Alaska, Guam, Hawaii and the Virgin Islands. Second mortgages also have limits, but the total loan value of the first and second mortgages cannot exceed this total.

FHA and VA Mortgages

The Federal Housing Administration (FHA) was established in order to assist lower to middle income consumers purchase a home. It allows Americans in this group access to federal insurance against losses for lenders who make their mortgages within specific rules and guidelines.

The Department of Veterans Affairs (VA) assists veterans and active duty personnel in purchasing their principal residence. Both of them, as well as the Farmers Home Administration, handle around one-fifth of residential mortgages in the country. For both of these programs, the standard debt and mortgage payment ratios will be more lenient.

Second Mortgages

A second mortgage is simply another loan against the property over and above the first mortgage. On default, proceeds are paid first to the primary lien holder, and only the leftover amount goes to the second mortgage. It makes them a larger risk, and the reason for their higher rates. As discussed already, one need for a second mortgage may be to stay within the 80 percent advance, or loan to value, ratio. This avoids added charges, and may make a second mortgage a less expensive alternative, and often for a much shorter period of time.

A second mortgage loan can also be helpful when purchasing a home with an attractive existing and assumable mortgage. It may cost you a fee (generally up to one point) but it could be a mortgage rate lower than those currently available. Newer mortgage notes almost always have a due-on-sale clause, which requires the seller to pay off the loan in full. In those cases, lenders may still allow the assumption but will adjust the interest to current market rates. Loans insured by the FHA or guaranteed by the VA are assumable with a fee and the credit approval of the buyer. In some States however, a seller may be more reluctant to allow their mortgage to be assumed, as they can remain liable in case of default for the full term of the mortgage even after the sale.

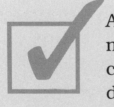

Assuming an existing mortgage will be your choice, it should only be done if it makes overall financial sense.

Depending on the amount, an assumable mortgage loan will leave a shortfall between the purchase price and existing loan. Rather than passing up this existing loan it may make sense to add a second mortgage for the shortfall of funds. While they are at a higher rate, a second mortgage (or line of credit) could be less costly. Of course this will always depend on how attractive the existing rate and terms really are. However, it only takes a simple calculation of the total payback with the fees versus obtaining a new loan at current rates to get the answer.

125% Mortgages

Yes, with the vast competition in the mortgage market, it is now actually possible to obtain a loan that is much more than the total value of the home. But like any other borrowing, just because it is possible, does not make it a good idea. Needless to say, most experts believe this is a very bad option for almost any consumer. After all, if an 80 percent mortgage is conventional or standard, owing 125 percent is usually not a wise option. Besides, the interest on this excess amount financed is not tax deductible and the loan payments will obviously be much higher. There is also a huge amount of financial pain should the house be sold. After the realtor fees, potential penalties and other costs, the amount left over will not come close to clearing the balance owing. It leaves a potential financial hangover for years to come which must now be refinanced as a personal loan, and at much higher interest rates and no room to negotiate.

HELOC

This is simply short for a Home Equity Line of Credit (HELOC). For renovations, a consolidation, or other reasons, many people believe this is their best financial alternative. As consumer loan interest is not tax deductible, these home equity lines of credit may allow interest deductibility if they are under the $100,000 maximum on equity indebtedness, and the total interest deducted is not in excess of fair market value of the home.

However, a larger number of people are now setting up their first mortgages as these lines of credit. Their costs are significantly less, sometimes as little as one point, which can even be negotiated. The challenge will be to get the correct quote of the margin (interest above the base rate) that a lender will charge. It is the percentage over the prime rate and not something most volunteer readily when you are shopping around. Lenders will refer to their introductory rate (for one to six months) but you are looking for the actual rate, based on your amount and your credit rating. That is also the time to obtain disclosure on fees which tend to be an annual charge, as well as a cancellation fee should the account be closed.

Their biggest risk is the exposure to interest rate changes. HELOC interest is calculated daily, which means any change in their base rate will immediately change the rate on this very large debt. They also do not come with caps, which most adjustable rate mortgages have as a ceiling. Their maximum rate can go up to 18 percent (16 in North Carolina), so make sure the HELOC is convertible into a fixed-rate loan.

Setting up a line of credit is usually done through a draw period ranging from five to 10 years where interest only payments are required. After that comes the repayment period of 10 or even 20 years where payments now increase, as they also need to repay the principal balance. Some, however have a requirement for total repayment on the date the actual draw period ends, which necessitates immediate re-financing, or payment in full at that point. While the ultimate goal is to be mortgage free, any line of credit which requires payments of interest only takes a lot of discipline to pay back since it will take large and fixed payments and a specific game plan to pay it off.

Mortgages for Condominium Units

A condominium development starts off with a mortgage by the developer. It covers the entire project, all apartments and the common areas of the complex. When one unit is sold, it is removed from the blanket mortgage so that clear title can be passed on to the purchaser. At that point the developer pays back a portion of the blanket mortgage to his or her lender until all the units are sold and the mortgage is fully discharged. Each owner of a condominium has title to their own unit, as well as some type of undivided interest in the common area.

The lender has the right to see the minutes of the condo board meetings and to enforce payment of the homeowner association dues. Typically, condominium mortgages also have a clause in the contract that require adherence to the rules and by-laws of the condo association. In every other way, the actual loan is the same as for other types of properties.

Your Other Options

In addition to some of these standard loan types there are many other options that are specifically designed to meet the needs of various groups of consumers. These range from loans that require no proof of income to others which do not calculate any ratios. Of course, anything out of the ordinary will generally come with higher interest rates, more points paid up front, or specific restrictions. For most people, these types of loans will likely involve the help of a professional mortgage broker who is well versed with all the options, pitfalls and surprises that may be involved.

Mortgage Insurance

With a down payment of less than 20 percent, lenders will almost always require the loan to be insured. It simply protects them in case of default, because of the smaller amount of equity. The benefit of mortgage insurance is that it allows consumers to purchase a home with as little as a three to five percent down payment, which would otherwise be impossible.

The cost of insurance will vary between lenders and States, so here again it pays to shop around and ask the right questions. The cost will also depend on the credit history of the buyer and the actual down payment, as these are two of the biggest risk factors. Insurers understand that someone with a larger down payment will be much less likely to default, and anyone with an excellent credit history has proven over a long period of time that they pay their bills.

A good starting point is to find a lender who deals with Genworth Financial for their mortgage insurance coverage. Their premiums are very competitive, and they are one of the leaders in the financial services industry. Genworth is not only involved in the communities they serve, but also believe very strongly in educating consumers and have received a number of industry "Integrity First Awards." From a Genworth University to home buyer resources, and a Center for Financial Learning in both English and Spanish, the company certainly believes in making a difference for their 15 million customers.

Insurance premiums are generally included in the monthly payments, although they can also be paid up front, or annually. Costs can range from $40 to $90 per month based on a median price of a single family home. The coverage insures the loan amount over 80 percent only and is reasonably inexpensive. For mortgages made under the Federal Housing Administration, the coverage is generally more expensive as it covers 100 percent of the loan.

To potentially avoid mortgage insurance, almost half of all purchases now involve some sort of piggyback financing. These are alternative ways to structure mortgage loans with less than a 20 percent down payment. For someone with a 10 percent down payment, this could become an 80-10-10 loan. It keeps the actual mortgage at 80 percent of the house value. The balance, which is the 10-10 part, would then be through a 10 percent second mortgage, or line of credit, and the 10 percent down payment. This avoids additional charges and fees, but it is always important to compare the cost of the second mortgage with the cost of mortgage insurance. Just avoiding some fees is pointless if the total interest on the second mortgage turns out to be more costly. After all, whether it is fees, points or interest, it's all money coming out of your pocket.

In all cases, federal law requires that mortgage insurance made after July 29, 1999 end automatically once the mortgage amount is reduced to 78 percent of the original house value. This does not apply to mortgages deemed high-risk, if you have been in arrears in the past twelve months, or to government-insured VA or FHA loans. By law, borrowers since August 1999 will also be advised at closing, and once each year, of their rights to cancel insurance coverage. Some States have laws that even apply to mortgages made before this date. Fannie Mae and Freddie Mac also have their own cancellation guidelines. With different rules and policies it is always worthwhile to contact your lender and ask if you are paying mortgage insurance, and specific regulations on how and when your policy can be terminated.

Paying the Points

Charging points, also known as discount points, is a way for lenders to collect some of their interest income up front. In return, they are willing to offer you a lower interest rate for the mortgage loan. One point is simply one percent of the total loan amount. A $100,000 mortgage charging two points will be a payment of $2,000 up front. But be careful that negotiating a better rate with a lender does not simply increase the points charged up front. As a general guide, if you have good credit and are not at maximum debt load, you may be able to negotiate a rate reduction of one-half to one percent and a one-point reduction in the fees. While HUD or VA guaranteed loans prohibit buyers from paying any points, for the rest, they will generally be charged.

The question then becomes whether to pay more points up front for a lower rate, or to get the points reduced, but pay a higher interest rate. It depends on whether you have the funds to pay these points and how long you plan to have the mortgage. While the points you pay are tax deductible in the year they are paid, it still involves putting up a whole lot of money. A general rule of thumb is that the longer you will have the loan, the more it makes sense to pay the points in exchange for a lower interest rate. After all, even a half percent over a very long time adds up quickly. On the other hand, if you only plan to be in the house for a few years, even an extra percent of interest will probably be less costly than points paid up front. Points may be also tax-deductible in the year they are paid. Once you have an idea of how long the loan will likely be around, just ask your lender to calculate the total payback with their lower rate and points up front, or a higher rate and reduced points.

Adjustable Rate Mortgages

These are the mortgage loans that can come with those very attractive rates that actually make you stop what you're doing and watch a commercial, or read an advertisement. But buyer beware – they are introductory or teaser rates designed to do just that. As the words imply, this is an interest rate that will be adjusted at some point. Whether you are considering refinancing, or obtaining a new mortgage, nobody knows with any certainty what interest rates will do in the future. Experts can make predictions, but they are not making your payments.

Adjustable Rate Mortgages (ARM), or hybrid adjustable mortgages, are available in a wide variety of terms ranging from 1, 3, 5, 7 or even 10 years. Because they are adjustable, they generally come with a lower interest rate and often include a convertible feature, which allows them to be changed to a fixed rate term after a specific period (often three years). ARMs generally adjust their rate every six or twelve months. However, it can also be as often as a monthly change depending on their specific terms and conditions. There can also be extended periods of time when interest rates are stable and mortgage rates don't change much at all. For anyone who knows they will be moving again in a few years, an ARM may save on interest-costs over the shorter term and with minimal risk. In fact, more than one-third of home loans are now structured in this way.

All rate adjustments correspond to fluctuations in the index which lenders use as their benchmark. Generally this is based on the six-month rate of treasury bills plus their mark-up.

In advertisements and loan documents this is called the index plus margin. When rates are falling, it means a reduced interest rate right along with it. When rates are on the increase however, the mortgage rate keeps going up as well.

But ARMs do have a limit on their potential interest increase. These are called rate caps and are set up for a specific time period to put a ceiling on their total rate changes. For those whose adjustment period is every six months, the cap is generally one percent. For annual adjustments, caps will be around two percent. An actual lifetime cap is the most critical feature to know before ever signing an ARM. It gives the maximum possible increase over the life of a mortgage and can range from three to six percent. That is definitely something to always know and consider in advance – just in case.

15 or 30 Year Mortgage?

Long term or short is a question that has a different answer for different sets of needs, risk tolerances, budgets and comfort levels. Nothing feels better than to have a long-term loan when rates are rising and to have the lowest possible payment. But they also come with higher interest rates, as lenders are risking their returns (interest income) over a much longer period of time.

But then maybe nothing feels better than to know the end of a mortgage is actually within sight. Or perhaps to know that more of your payments are going toward the principal each month and that the loan is being paid off in half the time. At the end of the day, only you can decide your risk tolerance or comfort level in possibly taking on a shorter-term mortgage loan with a higher payment. The payoff is huge if your goal is to be mortgage and debt-free. Interest deduction amounts aside, the best mortgage is still no mortgage at all.

That makes the question of your term the most important one of all. While many other term options are available, 15 or 30-year terms are still the most common ones.

A 30-year mortgage can get you:

• Into a home much more easily as a first time homeowner.

• The ability to carry other additional bills without exceeding your debt load maximum since the payments will be lower.

• The ability to also save for your retirement or investments as the payments may be more manageable with your income. Or you may have a better plan for the extra monthly savings somewhere else.

• A higher mortgage loan and a more expensive home, while still having a payment that fits your budget and debt load.

• A larger tax deduction. When you are paying a lot of interest, of course you will have a higher deduction, but this should not be your only consideration.

A 30-year mortgage can cost you:

• Through payments over a very long period of time.

• By having you counting on an increase in property values, instead of knowing you are paying down your mortgage quickly, no matter how market values change.

• Large penalties if you are planning to sell or move in the next few years. (In that case, you should always investigate an adjustable rate mortgage for any short period of time).

• A lot of interest. Especially in the first years of the mortgage, it can seem like nothing is reducing the principal.

A 15-year mortgage will certainly have higher payments. It may also make it more difficult to qualify for, since the monthly payments are higher. This might also make it more challenging to stay within the maximum payment ceiling of 28 percent, or the general guide of not having your total monthly payments exceed 36 percent of your gross income.

Is it worth paying off your mortgage in half the time? Only you can decide. But the decision should not be an automatic acceptance of a 30-year mortgage without weighing and exploring your options first. On a $100,000 loan using a rate of seven percent, without taking your tax deductibility into account, the following are some of the interest figures:

Your 30-year mortgage at $665 per month:

After year	Total paid	Interest paid	Principal paid	Balance
# 5	$39,918	$34,050	$ 5,868	$94,132
#10	$79,836	$65,648	$14,188	$85,812

You are only half way to paying off your balance after more than 21 years and the total you are paying will be $665 each month or $239,400.

Your 15-year mortgage at $899 per month:

After year	Total paid	Interest paid	Principal paid	Balance
# 5	$ 53,930	$31,343	$22,587	$77,413
#10	$107,860	$53,253	$54,607	$45,393

You have reached the halfway mark in just over nine years and the total you are paying will be $899 x 180 months or $161,820. Hopefully you've studied these figures a couple of times, as nothing could be more powerful than seeing this summary. It is something you can easily calculate with a printed schedule from your lender, some inexpensive software or from many Web sites before deciding on your term.

A printed mortgage schedule lets you track your progress and motivates you to accelerate your payments.

Just calculating the total amount you will be paying back is also very easy. Simply multiply your 15-year payment times 180 and your 30-year payment times 360. The difference between these two figures is your actual interest saving (before tax deductibility is taken into account).

Yes, it will save you a total of more than $77,000 in interest before tax deductibility is factored in. For that amount of money is it worth doing everything possible to avoid a 30-year mortgage? Only you can decide.

No, it won't be easy. It will mean higher payments and that often means an adjustment in your lifestyle. You may need to keep your bills under control or delay buying that cool truck you really wanted. Again, only you can decide if the huge interest savings are worth it. You also might not be able to purchase the perfect house you wanted, and may need to find one which is a little less expensive. After all, a $10,000 smaller mortgage will reduce your 15-year payments by around $90 a month.

A faster principal repayment will also reduce any cost of mortgage insurance. If the earlier example uses a 10 percent down payment, insurance is required. While it can be canceled once the balance gets to the 78 percent loan to value ratio, you first have to reach that point. On the 30-year example, that won't happen for almost nine years. On the 15-year mortgage, this will happen in less than three years. Even a $50 premium for six years less will save you more than $3,600 in fees.

Your Mortgage Obligations

Everything you must do is spelled out in many pages of legal size documents that you pay someone to walk you through. Those same forms specifically outline what you can or cannot do, and under what conditions default occurs. Most are standard mortgage terms and include requiring you to:

- Pay the payments on time each month – every month.
- Make your property tax payments when they are due (if not included in your payment to the lender already).
- Stay within your State and local rules, zoning and by-laws.
- Keep up the home, so the value does not go down and jeopardize the lender. Nobody is interested in whether you

want to re-paint the bathroom, but they do want you to fix structural damage and the like, which have a large impact on the value.

• Keep both mortgage loans up-to-date if you have a second mortgage, HELOC, etc. They are inter-connected, as they are both secured against the same property.

• Keep it insured – adequate insurance protects the lender in the event of a fire or other damage. The lender holds the mortgage and wants to make sure there is insurance coverage to restore the value of the property.

Refinancing Your Mortgage

Overall, refinancing your loan is exactly the same as obtaining a new mortgage from scratch. The only difference is that title of the property does not change. In total, there are around 75 million home-owning households in the United States, of which about 58 percent actually have a mortgage. With that many homeowners considering renovations, consolidations or just taking advantage of any rate reductions, refinancing is a major part of the mortgage loan field. It is estimated that even back in 2003, nearly 12 million loans were refinanced for over 2.27 trillion dollars, and a total interest saving of $31 billion according to the Federal Reserve.

Every person has his or her own justifications for refinancing. Everyone also has an opinion of whether it should be done at all, or whether it will save money over the long term. There are no right or wrong answers, but there are definitely some general guidelines and pointers to consider beyond the question of tax savings, which will also be different for every person.

Refinancing can often involve penalties and fees. They are charges which lenders collect if you want to refinance for any reason but are locked in to a fixed term. While they are not permitted under FHA or VA mortgages, every other loan could well charge them if you want to re-do your mortgage during the term. These penalties will vary between States and are different for each lender, but can generally be up to three percent of the unpaid balance or six months of interest charges on the outstanding amount. It is another reason to know these charges before ever signing a mortgage – just in case. Federal truth-in-lending legislation does require this information to be supplied at the time of the original loan application.

Penalties can also decrease the longer the loan has been open. Lenders make the bulk of their profits (interest) in the first five years and in the up-front points and fees. Therefore there may not be any penalties after the first five years, or lenders may be a lot more flexible.

A rough rule of thumb is that it could be a wise financial decision to refinance if rates decrease around one percent or more, especially for someone who will have their mortgage for some time to come. But the most important questions is still whether you are gaining ground, which always involves calculating the total payback. After all, having already paid five years on a mortgage very little has yet gone to principal. If the balance is now refinanced, and another 30-year cycle is started, the actual time to be debt-free will now be 35-years. If the term is reduced right along with a lower rate, the savings will become very significant and the length of payments is not stretched out. This is easily done by simply having the lender set up the new payments to match the original loan. Once again, it also pays to ask the right questions and to do the math. If the closing costs are $4,000 and the monthly savings are $133, it will take you 30 months to recover them ($4,000 total costs divided by the $133 savings each month) and to start seeing a benefit.

When it comes to consolidating debts, some of the drawbacks have already been discussed earlier. The total interest may be less and can now potentially be tax deductible. But these bills are now being paid back over a much longer period of time. Sometimes a drop in rates, or creating some breathing room from other bills, makes refinancing an attractive or necessary alternative, as long as you don't lose focus of the main goal of being debt-free. Nothing else will create as much financial freedom, savings, or peace of mind for you.

Paying More – Paying More Often

One of the most powerful ways to make a significant impact on your mortgage is to pay more, and more often than the basic payment. This is especially true for anyone with a 30-year mortgage. The first question to ask your lender is what your prepayment options are. The answers will vary widely, but most mortgages do allow you to put extra money toward the principal. After all, the more money you pay - the less interest, and the faster the end will arrive. Even with mortgages that claim to charge prepayment penalties, actually being charged a penalty is infrequent. It would simply be too costly and labor intensive to calculate and charge a penalty on a few extra dollars each month. It would cost the lender more to calculate and bill than they would make in extra income.

Anytime you owe less next month the interest will also be less. For many, their payment booklet or coupons already have a section that refers to additional payments, or additional principal amount. It is only a matter of adding some money and sending it in with a clear note that this is to go onto the principal and not set aside for the next payment. Loan payments always take the interest out first. After that, whatever is left goes straight off the balance. On a six percent mortgage over a 30-year term, even a small $25 or $50 each month quickly adds up in interest savings:

Prepaying each month:	Original loan amount of:			
	$100,000	$150,000	$200,000	$250,000
$25	$13,940	$14,606	$14,967	$15,192
$50	$24,570	$26,672	$27,880	$28,664

The greatest mortgage is no mortgage at all.

One of the most powerful and effective ways to make a big difference on the principal balance is to set up the payments on a bi-weekly basis. It simply takes your monthly payment, divides it by two, and has you paying half your monthly payment every two weeks. So on a $100 payment you would be paying $50 every two weeks. But for the year, you are now paying $1,300, instead of monthly payments which add up to only $1,200. It is a relatively pain-free way to actually make the equivalent of 13 payments.

If your lender cannot do this without fees or hassles, you can do it yourself by just sending an extra one-twelfth of a payment each month. It doesn't sound like much? Wonderful! Because it isn't a lot every two weeks, but quickly adds up. On a $100,000 loan at eight percent, it will save over $47,000 in interest!

Monthly payment: $735 and total interest of $164,155
Bi-weekly payment: $367 and total interest of $116,492

Increasing the frequency is one of THE most effective ways to reduce your total interest. No trick, no gimmick, no catch – just more money going toward the principal more often means less interest – it really is that simple. You do need to make sure your lender actually applies each payment immediately to get the interest savings, and does not wait for the second half of the month.

Of course, your loan almost always allows you to deduct the interest from your Federal income tax. So a five percent rate may have an effective rate of three or three and a half percent. This makes pre-paying your mortgage a good idea only after all your high interest debts are paid off first.

Chapter 8

Your Credit Bureau File

You can run, but you cannot hide when it comes to your credit history. Even 20 years ago, a move across the country meant a good chance of leaving behind some credit problems that lenders might not discover. Those days are long gone, much to the relief of all lenders because of centralized credit bureaus. Credit rating agencies are actually clearing houses of information. If you don't know them – they certainly know you. While there are over 1,000 credit reporting agencies, the largest are Equifax, TransUnion and Experian, and most consumers have a unique file with each company.

 The credit bureaus have over 150 million credit files and sell 50 million reports each year.

Credit bureaus do not actively gather facts and reports. They collect information from banks, credit card issuers and almost all other lenders. They do not rate customers, but accumulate, sort and sell factual information as a central clearinghouse. At regular intervals, tens of thousands of lenders simply exchange their data with the credit bureaus, which instantly update consumers' files with new accounts or fresh information.

Everyone who lends money uses the credit bureaus as a reference source. Lenders receive a reduced price to purchase files in return for exchanging their customer data. It means borrowers can stop wondering if their late payment won't be noticed or reported, or a repossession might not show up. It will, without doubt - and quite quickly. After all, your credit rating is your factual, detailed financial reputation and lenders and credit bureaus have much longer memories than debtors. Why should you care? Even something as simple as opening a checking account with a bankcard has the financial institution looking at your credit report. They're extending credit when they allow you to make withdrawals from your accounts without first putting a hold on deposits made through their machine.

What's In Your File

While files exist on almost every adult, the content is nowhere near as exciting as people think. It does not contain criminal records, asset lists or office gossip. It is only a library, which catalogues and distributes factual and credit related information. The content of files consists of various parts that include:

- Identification section – to locate and identify the person. It is the name, address, birth date and social security number.

- Payment history – the track record of accounts, including the amount borrowed, creditor, payment terms, current rating on an account, as well as its payment record in the past.

- Voluntary inquiry information – lists the companies with whom you have applied for credit and who have accessed your file and received the report in the past.

- Involuntary inquiries – this section shows all others who have looked into your report, where companies have updated their files, or obtained a basic profile before sending out pre-approved mailings. Inquiries by employers are also appear in this section.

- Public records – included here are bankruptcies, collections, foreclosures, suits, wage attachments (garnishees), defaults on government loans and judgments, as well as any secured loans and liens in most circumstances.

What A File Looks Like

A fictitious file will look somewhat like:

FN 00-007622-03-944   03/22/05
*WANTCREDIT,JAMES,L, KAREN   SINCE 02/12/96   FAD 01/12/05
  123 ANY STREET, YOURTOWN, CA 55555
  222 DIFFERENT AVE, YOURCITY, CA 44444
ES-INSTALLER, CA WORKALOT COMPANY
EF-LABORER, CA WORKALITTLE COMPANY
BDS-08/10/62   SS#: 111-11-1111

TRADE INFORMATION

Company	Date Reported	Date Opened	High Credit	Current Balance	Current Rating	Past Rating
*ABC VISA	04/05	02/96	2140	1164	current	
*RETAIL CARD	02/05	11/99	1000	200	90 days	60+days 11/03
BANK OF ANYWHERE	01/05	09/02	14500	10740	current	

VOLUNTARY INQUIRIES

DATE	INDUSTRY	DATE	INDUSTRY
02/19/05	BANK	12/14/03	RETAIL
04/07/03	RENTAL CO.	03/19/03	AUTO FINANCE
02/02/03	CREDIT UNION		

OTHER INQUIRIES

DATE	INDUSTRY	DATE	INDUSTRY
10/17/04	CREDIT CARD	06/10/04	BANK
04/14/05	DEPARTMENT STORE		

PUBLIC RECORDS & COLLECTION ITEMS

09/03 Collection $396   Satisfied 12/03

How To Read the Report

The first section is the place any computer looks for in finding the file. It contains the name, spouses name, followed by the *since date* showing how long the consumer has had a file. Lenders want to know how far back this customer's credit history goes. For this consumer, it is February of 1996. It then lists the current and previous address, birth date, social security number and employment information.

The second section is simply the summary of what is detailed from each of the creditors reporting. This is a Visa card opened in February of 1996 and last reported to the credit bureau in April of 2005. It has a limit (or highest credit) of $2,140 and a current balance of $1,164. The rating on this account is up-to-date. The past rating information is also very important to lenders. It shows the number of times the account has been 30, 60 or more days behind. For this card, it was once 60 days past due in November of 2003. The other two accounts are another small retail card and a bank loan with a balance of $10,740.

The third section shows the inquiry history. This is the summary of all lenders who have looked at the file and the dates of their inquiries. The voluntary section shows the date and industry where this customer has actually applied for credit. The other inquiry section tracks which companies have also reviewed the full file or a summary, as discussed already.

The final section of public records and collections shows that this customer had a collection in 2003 and it was satisfied (paid off or settled) in December.

How to Check Your Information

It is the right of any individual to review their credit file. Unfortunately, most are likely to check just after they've been declined for credit. With changes to the Fair Credit Reporting Act in late 2004, every individual is entitled to one free credit report per year from each agency. The reference section in the back of the book outlines the procedure to follow, who to contact, and how to obtain your report, and to correct any errors that were part of the decision to deny a credit account.

Like any other checkup, it is a good idea to review your file frequently to stay aware of the content, its accuracy and to prevent identity theft. The process involves contacting the credit reporting agencies, or the centralized contacts established by the Federal Trade Commission, and giving them some basic information and identification for security purposes. After that, the report will be mailed, along with an instruction sheet on how to read the report written in user-friendly language. It is definitely warranted to obtain all three reports from Equifax, TransUnion and Experian. Much of the information will be the same, but since the different reporting agencies deal with different lenders, some of their content can be unique to their report.

There are also companies who claim to supply free credit reports. However, they generally require you to subscribe to a monthly monitoring service. Be sure to compare prices, cancel your monthly charge immediately, or simply stick with contacting the three credit reporting agencies directly. You'll also need to be sure that your reports include your FICO credit score as it is an integral part of the credit information you'll need.

Mistakes To Look For

The most common errors are often housekeeping items on an ever changing and very fluid credit report. For the most part, these fall into some of the following categories:

- Spouse - This information can be outdated or incorrect. While it is not part of the rating, it can easily be updated.

- Current address – This is generated by the last inquiry. Before the file is accessed, the credit grantor enters the basic information, which locates the correct file and also uses it as the latest update. This information may have been entered incorrectly and is also easy to correct.

- Paid out accounts not up-to-date – It is possible that a computer burp, oversights or other errors can cause a paid down or paid in full account to be shown incorrectly. Any overstated payments and balances affect future borrowing. It causes the total debt and payments to be inaccurate and too high, which will matter on your FICO score. In these cases, the credit bureaus require proof that the account is paid in full and will contact the lender for verification. For these, it is also worthwhile to contact the actual creditor to re-input their information accurately.

- Collections not cleared - While a collection will stay on file for many years, there is a big difference between a paid and settled account, or a collection which is still outstanding. These items are usually debts that have been turned over to a collection agency, which focuses far more on the collection effort than updating the satisfactory payment information after the fact. Frequently the credit file is not updated after payment is made. It is critical that the status and balance of these items is accurate. With an open collection, there will almost always be a requirement to pay it in full before any loan is approved.

- Good credit references missing - It is anyone's right to have their credit file complete as well as accurate. When a loan or other account is missing, it is worth a request that the item be included in the file, especially for anyone with minimal credit references. It only makes sense to have as many positive references as possible, which includes accounts already paid in full over the past number of years.

How to Fix Stuff

Errors do happen, and with tens of millions of accounts, vast numbers of consumers have mistakes in their files. Often this is not a matter of blaming anyone, since it often starts with borrowers giving partial information, lenders not updating files correctly and ending with bureaus inserting something incorrectly. All files are the result of vast amounts of information gathered from many diverse sources. Horror stories do exist and make great headlines, as do examples of frustration in not getting a credit file corrected, even with all kinds of written documentation.

Various studies have shown that up to 40 percent of credit files can contain errors. This means that literally millions of individuals have a reason to review their files, and to do so before it becomes a problem. After all, you can never fix what you don't know. What is critical to remember is that lenders believe you are guilty until proven innocent. Every company believes in the accuracy of your credit file until it is corrected.

When a person is denied credit, the Equal Credit Opportunity Act requires lenders to mail a rejection letter called the adverse action letter. It is a very short and easy to read note that will always include the specific reason for the turndown. It will also have the name and contact information of the credit bureau which has supplied a credit report. That is the time when most people first realize there may be a problem in their file.

In all cases of a dispute, the credit bureaus need to be advised in writing. When documentation such as a receipt can be supplied it will speed up the research that will always be done. If someone disputes a specific item in the file, credit bureaus will investigate by contacting the original source for verification. If an error is found, the item is corrected or removed. Credit bureaus are required by law to fix the file within a reasonable period of time, which is normally considered to be 45 days or less. But like all good news, you wish references stayed much longer – like all bad news, you wish they would go away much sooner.

But if the information is accurate, it will stay in place. At that point, the only recourse a consumer has is to submit a short note into their file to outline another interpretation, or explanation of the facts. This consumer statement will have the individual's version and explanation of a disputed item.

One of the biggest preventative steps to avoid errors is by consistently using the same name on every application to reduce the chance of confusion with someone else. Variations such as Mike or Michael, Michael A. or Michael Andrew make referencing more difficult. The more common someone's last name, the wiser it is to consistently use a full first and middle name on all accounts and applications.

Reporting companies also obtain information from bankruptcy registers, court records and collection agencies. Often these files are referenced by only a debtor's name and address. Their information rarely includes birth dates or social security numbers, which means lots of room for error when this is added to a report. It is the reason incorrect information is almost always negative in content.

There are specific rules that govern the credit bureaus conduct and operations. The most important one is that all files remain confidential and that your full report can only be accessed by someone you have authorized to investigate your credit. In fact, pulling your file without authorization can result in fines up to $5,000 or even imprisonment. Specific rules and rights are part of the Fair Credit Reporting Act and include the rights to:

- Be advised of the nature and source of information collected and held in your file.

- Have your credit score provided with your report for a "fair and reasonable" fee as determined by the FTC, along with a list of four factors that have adversely affected a score.

- Receive your report free of charge each year.

- Know who has accessed your report within the past six months (or two years in the case of employment inquiries).

- Have incorrect, outdated or incomplete information investigated and removed when it is proven to be incorrect or unable to be verified.

- Assurance that your report is not sold or accessed by anyone who does not have a legitimate authority.

- Have negative information removed from your file in seven years at longest (and 10 years in the case of a bankruptcy).

- Have a statement of dispute included in your file where a matter cannot be resolved.

It is sad, but true, that in the last decade the Federal Trade Commission (FTC) received more complaints related to credit reporting issues and abuses than all other complaints combined. When all other avenues have failed, they are the agency to contact. Information for the FTC is in the reference section of the book.

 **Information in credit files is generally retained for six years.**

Items in credit files stay on record for various lengths of time, and can vary by State. Their general parameters are as follows:

- Inquiry by a creditor or employer - up to two years from their date and always a minimum of two years for employment inquiries.

- Judgments - purge at longest, seven years from date filed.

- Collections - both paid and unpaid stay a maximum of seven years from their date of last activity supplied.

- Trade items - no actual statue of limitation exists for positive information, however credit bureaus generally drop them from files within five years of the date of last activity.

- Credit cards - always update as a credit card continues to stay active. Missed payments showing a past due record will drop on or before seven years of the transaction.

- Bankruptcy - ten years after the date of discharge.

- Debt management plans purge after seven years or less.

- Tax liens, U.S. government insured and guaranteed student loans – are dropped seven years from the date the lien is paid in full.

Credit Repairs

The most important point to understand is that no outside agency can repair someone's credit rating. In fact, credit bureaus won't even accept communications from third parties unless there is a notarized power of attorney. These agencies cannot fix something, change it, or make a credit problem disappear. Ads with these promises prey on consumers in the hope of somehow turning back the clock and operate on a fee for service basis. They require money up front for the hope and promise to change or fix a credit rating.

Credit repair firms market their services in two ways. The first is to suggest that a written notation be placed in the credit file. It is something any consumer can do without charge by simply contacting the credit bureaus. The second avenue is advising consumers to flood agencies and lenders with dispute letters and calls. This is another approach that will have no effect. So it is almost always just the money up front part that happens. Equifax says it best when they state: "Our mandate includes a commitment to protection of the credit industry by assiduously maintaining file integrity." While laws require disclosure and force these repair agencies to supply a written contract and specific outline of what their clients rights and obligations are, they cannot make people smarter consumers.

 The only guaranteed 'fix' for credit repairs is time and a consistent payment of other bills on time – every time.

From time-to-time a portion of the population experiences credit problems for one reason or another. The main area of concern revolves around the issue of how severe the problem really is or was. Missing one payment each year on a credit card is vastly different from having a repossession, bankruptcy or major write-off. These three are the most serious credit defaults. Any of these will prevent borrowing for some time to come. Yes, mitigating circumstances do matter, but not in the case of these defaults. The reason or explanation for these is of very little interest to a lender. Their view is that a creditor did not get paid back – either on time, or ever, in those circumstances.

Many people have a story that they believe is totally accurate about a cousin's friend or someone else. These stories almost always revolve around this person, after a serious credit problem, immediately getting some kind of unsecured credit again. Things are never as simple as they appear, or there would be very little reason for anyone to repay their debts. In fact, why would anyone pay his or her loans if the debt can just go away and another loan obtained without hassle?

After all, lenders rely on making a profit and fully expect to be paid back on time. To make sure they know as much information as is possible, they rely on credit reports for a full picture of all past credit references – both good and bad.

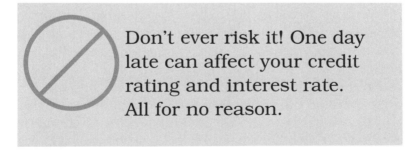

Don't ever risk it! One day late can affect your credit rating and interest rate. All for no reason.

Bad credit references affect credit ratings to various degrees just as a minor speeding ticket is treated differently than a major moving violation. This causes a chain reaction, which can prevent or restrict future borrowing. This is largely because of the effect on a FICO score, which will be discussed in the next chapter. In the worst cases, after seven years at most, the reference is deleted entirely. Another strong motivation to maintain a clean report is that a majority of employers use it as part of their hiring checks. Financial behavior is part of what an employer may consider for many positions.

What are Credit References?

Perhaps equally important is an understanding of what is not recognized as a credit reference. This list includes utilities, telephone bills and rental payments. Also not accepted are references from cellular phone carriers, self-financed car lots, lay-away plans, arrangements with doctors, or bank overdrafts.

The only time these become credit references is when they are not paid, and reported as collections or written off accounts. The only useable credit references are those from formal lenders. They range from financial institutions, credit card issuers and finance companies as well as auto finance firms such as Ford Motor Credit or Chrysler Financial.

Another shock for many people involves having a loan in the name of another individual, which is called a conversion loan. The loan is made under the name of another person because the original applicant had significantly bad credit that did not qualify him or her to be added on the loan documents. This means someone else fronted the loan, and is something that happens often, especially for the purchase of vehicles. No matter who is making the payments, the credit rating only goes to the person whose name appears on the loan. Not every lender explain that subtle but huge difference between conversion and cosigning. It often becomes a rude awakening, but only two or three years later when the process starts all over again, since no credit was rebuilt at all with this type of loan. Simply put – if your name isn't on the loan, you're not getting a credit rating for it.

It is also a common misconception that cosigners are only signing to help out. In fact, a cosigner is just as liable for the total debt and payments as the borrower. The credit bureau will also have the full loan information, good or bad, on the cosigner's report.

Chapter 9

Your FICO Score – It Matters a Lot

Perhaps a better name for this chapter is how do they really figure out so quickly if I'm approved? Well, this is where lenders use a numerical score on each application to make important credit decisions very accurately, quickly and in large quantities. All lenders use some sort of system to help predict what risk they might be taking on. Many have an internal system, while others use the FICO score from each credit report.

 A credit score is just a numerical representation of someone's creditworthiness.

Imagine hundreds of thousands of applications for credit cards without these computer-scoring systems and guess how long it would take to receive an answer on an application? With their massive volume and rapid turn-around requirements, credit card issuers have always been the leaders in this field. Between the ranges of easy approvals and obvious turndowns lies the largest and potentially most profitable group of applications. The credit card market has also become saturated. Good credit risk customers have their preferred cards and don't switch in sufficient numbers to gain more market share for another issuer.

On the other extreme, a certain percentage of consumers either don't want credit cards, or don't qualify for them. That leaves the challenge of building an expanding base of cardholders from the shrinking group that is left. If they lend to more risky applicants, they can get a lot more customers, but at a cost. An increase in their numbers results in more volume and more interest income. But it has to be measured against the chances of higher write-offs, bankruptcies and collection costs. Hence, the development of scoring systems which really do predict losses to within a fraction of a percentage point. But even small fractions still amount to many millions of dollars for every lender.

From banks to finance companies, every lender relies on one system or another. It takes almost all discretion out of deciding on an approval or turndown if it doesn't meet their minimum requirements. Yet nobody is declined based on that alone, but always on the underlying factors that create the (low) score.

Most people become uneasy at the initial thought of their credit application being handled by a machine and not a person. Quite the opposite is true. Long gone are the days of credit personnel relying on intuition and experience. Any credit officer that had recent collection problems with a roofer, for example, is unlikely to approve anyone else in that same occupation for a long time, no matter what the next one's credit rating. Previous manual systems also tended to stereotype against divorcees (of both sexes), certain occupations or lifestyles, and often against women. None of that ever enters into scoring systems. Besides, Congress passed the Equal Credit Opportunity Act to originally end discrimination against women, as well as others based on color, race, religion, sex, age, marital status or place of national origin.

Who Cares?

If you had two friends who wanted to borrow money from you, and you knew with a statistical certainty that one would pay you back and the other might not, would you want that information to make a decision? That is the reason for your FICO score which all lenders use as one of their main tools in evaluating your credit worthiness. It was developed by the Fair Issac Company in the 1950's (hence the acronym FICO) and is software used by all three credit bureaus as a uniform system.

Yes, your entire credit history is actually reduced to a three digit number ranging from the 300s to the 850s. Until 2001, this score was one of the most closely guarded secrets in the credit industry. Today, it is something every person needs to know before ever starting a loan, credit card, or mortgage application. While each lender has different criteria, a score below their internal cut-off will have many lenders declining an application, or certainly charging a higher interest rate. It works and everyone uses your FICO score. It is a quick and accurate predictor of your credit worthiness, but it is only one of the tools. A high score simply indicates an excellent credit risk, but does not confirm employment, income or a host of other factors.

Your FICO score is the key tool used to make billions of credit decisions each year, as well as the determining factor of the interest rates you will be charged for many types of borrowing. According to Fair Issac's own information, a sample mortgage of $150,000 had the following affect on the interest rate when compared to a score of 720 or higher:

A score of:	Extra interest costs over a 30-year mortgage:
700-719	$ 4,320 (a 0.12 percent higher rate)
675-699	$ 23,040 (a 0.66 percent higher rate)
620-674	$ 64,800 (a 1.81 percent higher rate)
560-619	$106,200 (a 2.92 percent higher rate)

With these staggering differences in rates, the Fair Credit Reporting Act was amended in late 2004. Mortgage lenders are now required to provide, without charge, the credit score and up to four key factors which adversely affect an individual's score. Lenders must also advise consumers when their rate is materially different from the best rates available to others. It is important to point out however, that a FICO score alone does not necessarily determine the interest rate. Factors such as income, down payments, debt load or other financial data can also be part of the interest rate. It is another reason to always shop around and explore your options.

The decision made by each lender is where to place their cut-off before they'll charge a higher rate or simply turn down an application. At what point will the largest number of applicants be approved without too much credit risk or collection problems down the road? Or what accounts do they say yes to, but at a higher interest rate? After all, economies of scale always dictate that any overhead costs or risks are much easier to absorb over a larger number of accounts. How do people score? According to Fair Issac about 20 percent of the population fall into these five categories: 620 or less, 620-690, 690-740, 740-780, or higher than 780.

Absolutely nothing else is as powerful as understanding the implications of a lower score than the interest approximations from the previous chart. Now do you understand in real terms how important your FICO score really is?

 Your FICO score is totally within your control—once you know how it works.

Changing Your Score

Both negative and positive factors influence a score, but each can vary in how much impact it has. For someone with a long credit history, a small negative such as missing one payment, will have only a minor impact.

Factors that can lower a credit score:

• The length of credit history – The longer the better, because it shows a stronger track record. It is something lenders check in evaluating how credit has been handled over many years. An ideal credit history has over 20 years of information. Five years is considered short, while a credit history of two or three years is generally too little. How the account has been paid is important, but also how long it has been open.

• Credit dealings – The larger any previous loan was, the better. The high credit shows the amount other lenders have advanced in the past. It includes the limit on credit cards, fixed loans and other borrowing. Lenders look to see whether they are going into a territory where the customer has never been. Only having $1,000 high credit will keep the credit score quite low. A score is also reduced when lenders report to the credit bureau that payments have not been made on time. They want to see that others have been paid back over time, on time, all the time.

• Number of major credit cards – Some are good, while too many cross the line. Generally any number beyond three or four starts to negatively impact a score. Also taken into account is the length of time since the last account was opened – the longer they have been in existence, the longer the track record on file.

Factors that can raise a credit score:

• The payment history – Simply put: no arrears, no collections, judgments or other negative references on a file. Of course, missing a single payment is not as serious as missing them to a number of accounts. Lenders understand that statements can be misplaced and the mail can be delayed. What makes it much more serious is a second or third consecutive missed payment.

• The use of credit – Higher balances will lower a score, while lower balances will reflect in a higher score. Credit can be used a lot each month, but when those accounts are paid off or greatly reduced, it positively impacts a score. Higher balances can lead to living beyond someone's means and possible future problems.

When the score is calculated, the credit decision is applied very simply. The applicant is most often approved or rejected on whether a minimum cut-off has been met. While a specific score may be acceptable to one lender, it may not be sufficient to approve the application somewhere else. Lenders have different requirements, risk tolerance and lending objectives that reflect what they will approve or decline in an application. They do know that these scores work. A study some years ago showed a one in nine chance that a mortgage would become over 90 days past due below a certain score. When the score was one-third higher, this chance dropped to one in almost 1,300. If it were your money, wouldn't you want better odds of being paid back?

The underlying reason for any credit decision is specific information such as job, income, debt load, too little credit or any host of other factors. Since a low score is the result of something derogatory or missing, those factors are used as the reason for the rejection of the application, or for charging a higher interest rate.

 One major credit card with a good limit, paid over many years, creates one of the best credit scores possible.

While lenders look to a broad list of factors to make their decisions, your FICO score involves only the information in your credit file. Negative information, such as arrears, or a judgment, will lower your score, while an up-to-date payment history and a reduced debt load will increase your score. The importance of any one factor depends on how much (or how little) information is in the file already. For the average individual a score involves:

• 30% for amounts outstanding on your loans, credit cards or other accounts. In this category, the software compares your credit limits to the amounts you owe. So moving one credit card to another, or combining two accounts, does not lower your total debt and will have little affect on your score, even though it may save you some interest. For anyone with a credit card it is unlikely that the FICO score will ever use a zero balance. Lenders report at various times, so it is likely that your last statement will be used in calculating the score. This section also considers how many accounts you have (back to the issue of having a large number of credit cards for no reason – and closing them properly, not just cutting them up). Do remember that cards with no balance actually lower your debt percentage versus your available credit. There are many reasons to cancel a credit card, just don't do it simply to increase your score.

- 15% for the length of your total credit history. Lenders and your FICO score love to see a very long history of credit. Unfortunately, this is generally a challenge for younger people or those with only recently established credit. It considers how long specific accounts have been open and the time since you last used those open accounts.

- 10% for any new applications. Are you on track to increase your debt? For this section, the software considers the applications for new accounts over the past year. But it does know the difference between shopping around for one particular loan or a number of different types of accounts. It also weighs how many of your accounts are new when compared to the total you already have. After all, more credit, and very recently, can often be a sign of increased debt later.

- 35% for your entire payment history on file. This includes all your past payment records which stay on file for approximately five to seven years. Of course, any arrears are a sure-fire way to reduce your score very quickly, as will any judgment or collection. But as was discussed already, a missed credit card payment three years ago will not have the same affect as two months arrears on your vehicle payment last year. The older the information, especially when new and positive ratings are in place, the less important it is. That means your entire history is taken into account, and any old problems that you may have forgotten are still impacting your score until they are dropped entirely. What matters today, and moves your score, is to make your payments on time – every time.

- 10% for the types of credit you have. What is the mix of credit you are using? Are you relying only on credit cards, or is it a combination of a personal loan, cards and a vehicle payment? While it is a small factor in your score, it may not be a good idea to have open credit accounts that you don't need or use.

For anyone with a long credit history, closing an extra credit card, or paying off an account, will generally have a positive impact on their score. For someone with a shorter credit history, it may be wise to keep the longest running account open since it also has the longest track record.

Even knowing a score today may not necessarily help next month, since it constantly changes and evolves as creditors report new updates. A general guide is that a score above 680 will give you a good interest rate, while a lower score will generally be charged subprime rates and anyone below about 550 would not be approved.

Sometimes knowing the score also raises more questions than it answers. There is no printed scoring sheet, which would just show you that a new credit card lowers your score by a certain number of points. But you will always have an idea if you're making progress with your score, or taking a step backwards by increasing the number of accounts, taking on additional payments, or missing payment. Whatever steps you take to make some progress in increasing your score, do remember that your efforts will take 60 or 90 days to show up. It will always take that long after paying off some bills or reducing accounts, before this information filters itself through to the credit bureaus and your FICO score.

Credit scoring is validated and here to stay. The original three C's of credit were character, capacity and collateral. All of these are outdated today and have evolved into the new three C's of credit: computers, credit bureaus and your credit score.

Chapter 10

Budget Stuff

 A budget cannot become a straitjacket or a "to the penny" rule book. It should be a game plan to celebrate, not a reason for fights.

Let's be honest. Perhaps a few people out of a hundred do a budget and actually follow it –and odds are you're not one of them. The vast majority of people feel they work hard for their money and want the freedom to spend some of it without feeling guilty or accounting for every dime. This is not a book about budgeting – although there are many excellent sources available. Unfortunately, they can become tedious or use examples that can be quite unrealistic. Yes, anyone that cuts out one coffee a day could save thousands of dollars over the years, but that money never shows up, does it? Maybe skipping the fancy coffees just makes it possible to buy some lottery tickets Friday night.

So instead of a budget, would it be better to call it a Financial Reality Check and just do it every six months? That simply involves filling in the list of assets (hopefully growing) and liabilities or debt (that should be shrinking). Then it can be compared to the last one you completed to see if you are making progress, or falling backwards.

The choice is yours, and either option is fine. As long as you do something to set a game plan and are able to measure progress in specific ways, it's worth the effort. How much energy would you spend on getting a raise? Well, having a critical look at your expenses and your budget is even more profitable, because any raise may also increase taxes, but only a small amount of extra income. That same effort in reducing interest, fees and expenses pays off in much bigger ways – for a lot more money.

Nobody can have a plan of where to go if they have no idea where they're at right now. Vagueness will not do it, so force yourself to be specific. That means some form of budget which has to be in writing and include everything – especially those once a year bills like car insurance, school fees and the likes. You need a game plan for those annual bills as well. They are not a surprise, so be ready. Doing a budget also cannot be done over dinner or while watching TV. It will take a little time, thought and effort. Then, just like following a diet, you will need the discipline to follow it through and the results will be awesome.

Some form of budget, and writing down a full list of debts, is often the hardest step for many. It shows a black and white written acknowledgment of reality. It points out where all that income is really going and how little is left at the end of the month. That's the reason to get mad at yourself - to change things around, to get back in control and to take charge of your money instead of the other way around. You also have to believe in yourself, that you can do it, and that anything is possible.

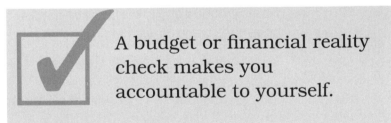

A budget or financial reality check makes you accountable to yourself.

The only way to achieve concrete results, little by little, is to always have a game plan. It applies to budgeting just as much as financial success in your life after debt. The common denominators include:

- knowing specifics and details

- always doing it in writing

- having a concrete time-line for getting it done

- knowing your game-plan for achieving your goals

- sticking to your plan – no matter what

- staying focused on the plan and being committed every day. Don't lose sight of the goal line.

And the great thing is that it is yours to do or not do – follow or ignore – any way you see fit. After all, nobody else cares as much about your money as you do. You will definitely need to be realistic and stay motivated. Only with a reasonable budget and a specific and important goal are you likely to succeed. Yes, there will be many times when you say to yourself that it's no big deal, it's only five bucks. Added together, it is a very big deal and a lot of money. But if a budget or an occasional Financial Reality Check is something you choose to, here are some basic points:

- Complete the budget at the back of the book just to get a handle on where your money is going right now. Specifics, honesty, reality and details matter – the more you guess or leave out, the less useful it becomes.

 Finding ways to reduce every bill pays off in big ways. Make it a game not a pain.

- Shave something off every bill: Each bill, just this month, gets reviewed with a microscope. The goal is to find some way to reduce each and every one. It is possible, but it will take a little creative thinking and probably asking some people at work, church, or in your family for ideas. Here are some examples:

Do you need call display and other phone add-ons, or do you just like to have them? The decision is yours, but it can reduce the bill if you choose. Check your service charges or package on your bank accounts. Are you paying the basic fee, or a number of other charges too? It probably means that your package does not meet your needs and should be changed. Plus, you'll likely have a number of charges for using the nearest bank machine for a fee, instead of your own. When you've set your spending money for the week, these *convenience* charges will disappear, plus you will be adjusting your extra service charges. For most, this change alone can easily be $20 to $30 each month.

Is your overdraft really necessary? Do you know the interest rate and charges each month? What are the service fees and interest when paying your insurance monthly, instead of annually? Yes, every bill can be reduced. All of them are important – but none of those companies are entitled to any more of your money than absolutely necessary.

 Want to save money, lower your payment and better your coverage? Get a comparison of your whole life insurance policy with a term policy.

What are you paying versus getting from your life insurance policy? According to the Wall Street Journal, half of all cash reserve (whole life or universal life) policies are dropped within the first seven years. After the fees, commissions and penalties in the early years, there will be almost nothing left in that hoped for cash value. You may want to avoid these policies altogether and check out some much less expensive alternatives.

• Forget the past: Never mind figuring out how many snacks or lunches you had last month. Start fresh and give yourself an allowance for *me* money each week. If you're in a relationship, you both get your own money – plus you will have to include some extra if you have kids. It is yours for the week to spend or save, as you see fit. What does it include? You have to set the rules. Are groceries and gas part of this money, or is that different? Your snacks and night out are definitely a part of the *me* money. So now you can leave your credit and debit cards at home. You have your money for the week. Anything else is now a planned expense. When you go on a long trip you pack differently than a workday right? This is the same – pack your wallet different for a shopping trip than a normal weekday. The rest is up to you. If you spend it all by Thursday – you will quickly be able to tell if you're serious about your debts. You can suffer the consequences for the rest of the week, or get some more money out of your account – it's all up to you. There are dozens of ways to cheat. Just loading up on junk food while shopping for groceries, instead of using the *me* money is just one great way of cheating yourself.

Is this just a waste of time? It depends on your attitude, priorities, goals and determination. The first step is to get over that *what's the use* mentality. Your entire debt mountain may be too big to climb right now. But as you will read in the next chapter, focus on one or two of your bills only and all of a sudden that $20 or $30 saved in a number of places starts to become a lot more important.

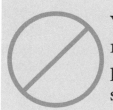
Your budget is not meant to reduce your spending one place just to add it somewhere else.

Chapter 11

Dealing with Debt

If you're broke, stressed out about your financial situation, or couldn't ever afford to miss a single paycheck – welcome to the club, as you're certainly not alone. It is just not something anyone really likes to admit, or talk about. It's sad but true that the last thing we ever want to say out loud is that we can't afford something, or that we're in trouble, isn't it?

Debt creeps up on you little by little, here and there for one reason or another. The balances get higher, the minimum payment moves up, one account gets used to cover another, the car needs repairs, the vacation is important but goes on a credit card and so on. Savings become less, IRA or 401(k) contributions are delayed or reduced just this year, and sometimes savings are used to pay some bills – just this once.

Debt is a silent killer that starts choking you, your lifestyle and your ability to maneuver. It is something most people already realize. After all, an Ipsos-Reid survey some years ago showed that over 90 percent of people listed paying down debt as their top financial goal. Debt stops savings and starts reversing years of hard work and discipline to build them up. The minimum payments creep up without much notice until one day – maybe not for quite a while – the juggling stops working. It might be a couple of weeks off work, unexpected medical or repair bills, taking Christmas shopping way over budget, or a host of other reasons.

Then it becomes a panic, but it is often already too late. *I never saw it coming.* Yes you did – perhaps you just chose to ignore it. Maybe it was optimism that things would turn out OK, or that you could manage and find a way. It may be fine for many years to come; it's just that every lender is making money off you except yourself. Around 20 to 30 percent off the top for taxes, to pay groceries, utilities and the likes, then pretty much turn the rest over to payments. Yes, most of it is in interest, but at least treading water is better than sinking. When did that become living and not just coping?

"We are likely to produce a nation of credit drunks."
— Former U.S. Senator William Proxmire

As you're reading this chapter and thinking about your personal game plan, it is important to stay aware of the impact of future interest rate changes as well. While we are not likely to see 15 or 20 percent rates again, they will certainly increase from their recent historic lows. How ready are you for any future increases?

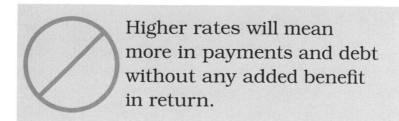

Higher rates will mean more in payments and debt without any added benefit in return.

Higher rates will not necessarily affect all of your debt immediately. The mortgage, if it is a fixed rate, will not be due for renewal. Nor will credit cards always change with each prime increase – they are high enough already. However the following will give you a good idea of the real cost of any potential increase in rates. Like all bills, more interest also has to be paid with after-tax income. For these examples, the real income needed is shown based on a 20 percent tax rate. How ready are you to perhaps spend $200 or more on extra interest payments if you add new debt, refinance or just watch as your current accounts start to increase their interest charges?

Debt amount:	Income needed to pay the extra interest:	
	3% rise in rates	4% rise in rates
$ 15,000	$ 31	$ 41
$ 30,000	$ 61	$ 83
$ 50,000	$103	$139
$ 75,000	$154	$208
$100,000	$205	$276
$150,000	$308	$415

(assuming a current average rate of 8% and rising from there)

Building Financial Success

Financially successful people have no real secret. They just do what others don't want to do, or find hard. They limit expenses, spend within their means, borrow only for assets that grow and not consumable debt, limit their credit card use, ask the right questions and pay themselves first by having some savings on hand. Nothing mysterious, but a challenge for many to learn.

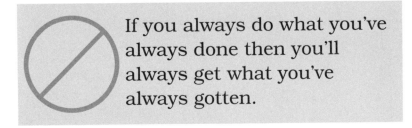

If you always do what you've always done then you'll always get what you've always gotten.

Unfortunately, it also can be a catch-22. The largest percentage of increased consumer debt comes from those most affected by economic changes, layoffs, outsourcing and downsizing. Debt is increasing twice as fast for individuals earning less than $25,000 than high-income earners. Plus they generally have debts with higher rates and less collateral on assets that could be sold to pay off accounts – hence the catch-22.

This is the place where we could quote a ton of statistics of what the average person owes, what the average credit card balance is, and so on. Unfortunately, you aren't the average. You are unique and your circumstances are unlike anyone else's.

Your income is not average and neither are your challenges, specific bills, which accounts you carry, what their interest rates are, or what your own hurdles and challenges may be.

Two statistics are worth knowing: 1.6 million – which is the approximate number of bankruptcies a year. But that figure is actually over 2.1 million people since many bankruptcies involve both husband and wife, plus the figure of over two trillion dollars, which is the total amount of consumer debt in this country. How much of that is yours?

What's happening for many people is that things are getting worse and not better. Credit counseling agencies are now just as busy in November and December. Unusual, since almost all consumers want their credit available at least through the Christmas shopping season.

The slippery slope of excessive debt can also result in real trouble with even a minor or temporary reduction in income. This results in more minimum payments to stall as long as possible, more arrears when only priority bills can be paid, and credit starts to be seen as a temporary bridge or substitute income. Plus we are now at the point where financial problems are the number one cause of male suicides.

When you want anything badly enough, you'll always find a way to make it happen.

Just like falling into a hole is easier than getting out of it – getting into debt is also much easier than turning things around. The first step is to stop adding to your debt load, and to stop making things worse. After all, consumer debt has more than doubled in the last 10 years. No wonder when in today's cashless society it is possible to spend thousands of dollars a day and never touch any real money. A couple of forms to purchase your stereo and no money down for a vehicle – just sign here. If that doesn't happen, there are still credit and debit cards that also contribute to piling on the debt or overdraft, and not a single $20 bill has physically left your pocket.

Is There Good Debt?

Is there such a thing as feeling OK about having some debts? Well, yes and no. The ultimate goal for everyone is to be debt-free. But until that day arrives, there is such a thing as good borrowing, if absolutely necessary. There is also debt that becomes more like a bad hangover after only a short time.

Good borrowing or debt	Bad borrowing
Getting out on your own	Wedding
For a vehicle	Furniture & appliances
For a house or condo	Holidays
For one credit card	Stock market tips
For an IRA or 401(k) (sometimes)	For others (cosigning)
For education (within limits)	Want to have things
For a real emergency (you decide)	One credit card used
Consolidating high bills – once!	to pay another

If you are not a homeowner, what exactly is stopping you from buying a house? For most renters it is the down payment, debt load, or closing cost obstacles, right? What are you paying on finance, credit card or loan payments right now? Think of that money as standing between you and the dream of getting your own home. Without some, or all of those bills, you wouldn't have the debt load and could easily save the down payment and closing costs. So get mad and get rid of them!

If you already own a home, a mortgage is often good debt. It allowed you to purchase the house and is helping to build equity over time while the mortgage is being paid off. It can also give you some interest deductions and the house is likely to increase in value. However, to re-mortgage can cross the line of taking on bad debt. After all, the goal is to be mortgage free. If it is done to consolidate other bills, it should definitely be a one-time occurrence. As this can be a step backwards, make sure the other accounts are closed and the re-mortgaged old bills are paid off quickly to get back on track sooner, rather than later.

Not everything in this chapter will apply to you – hopefully none of it. But if it does, you have just read the biggest lesson to learn. Get mad at yourself and start turning things around. Just like stopping a train, it will take a long time and a lot of effort and discipline. But once it's stopped – to go in a different direction will be much easier, and you will never look back. Are you worth it? Are you prepared to do more of what works to get what you want – and do less of what doesn't work? Will you commit to a long-term plan?

Borrowing Less

Your game plan should always start by stopping. Stopping to borrow more money, or certainly to borrow less, pay a little more and save a little extra. Overall, there are some basic steps to review. Some of them may be obvious, but many people still aren't aware of all their options.

• Change your habits and start using a debit card instead of a credit card.

• Is there a way to increase your income? A part-time position on a temporary basis, overtime, or any other options?

• Are there any savings around? It might sound silly but many people carry large credit card balances while having a savings account or certificate of deposit paying very little interest.

• Is there anything you can do without?

• Can you switch to a low interest credit card, transfer your old balance to it, and terminate the old card?

• Are there any assets you can sell – second car, etc?

• Are you able to move high interest debt to a line of credit?

• Can you cut back? Lunch out every day, or perhaps going out to dinner less often? Every bit will help – don't minimize the impact of 10 bucks here or there. You'd be surprised how quickly it adds up – if you choose.

- Do you have a whole life (cash value) insurance policy? Are you able to get a loan against it? If you can't, why have this expensive type of coverage? Saving through a life insurance policy can be a very bad and expensive financial strategy. A term policy will always be less expensive and frees up cash in your budget that is better spent or invested elsewhere.

- Can you get a bank loan against your vehicle?

A first good step is to start treating your credit cards like writing checks and faithfully tracking each charge. This avoids the surprise of seeing the actual total on the monthly statement. Almost everyone estimates their monthly balance too low or couldn't even name the last five things charged on their card. Sit down right now and write down what you think this month's balance will be – chances are you will guess on the low side by a surprisingly large amount. When it comes to your debts, it is not the time to be overly optimistic. An American Bankers Association survey found that the typical consumer thought it would take two months to pay off Christmas shopping bills, while their average was really around six months.

It All Starts With a Game-plan

Your budget puts things into perspective and shows where the money is going each month. Getting started on paying off your debt means having a plan of attack. Make the plan, then work the plan – no matter what. Some points that make it a little easier might be:

- Don't focus on your total debt – it is depressing and you will get that *what's the use* feeling.

- You gave your word that you'd pay it back – keep it if at all possible. Explore all options, utilize all the resources and debt counseling tools at your disposal. When all is said and done, you will feel great that you accomplished it.

- Share your goals with others – it is not a reason to be embarrassed – it's a reason to be proud. The more people who know, the more likely you are to stick with it, and to have a large cheering section that care about you and will support you. You won't know until you try.

- Make a plan and work the plan. Just like a budget, working the plan means discipline and sticking to it.

- One thing at a time – pick your smallest bill and tackle it first. It will create the feeling that you can do it – it will give you a sense of accomplishment and it's the smallest mountain to climb. Make your minimum payments on all the other accounts and dump everything else on the one that you have picked. Get it set up on your web banking, or through your ATM. If you skip this step you can only pay once a month when you have a statement to mail along. You want to be able to pay lots and pay often. The key is to send that extra 20 bucks when you have it. Don't put it aside hoping, wishing, and thinking it will still be around when next months' statement arrives – chances are, it won't be.

Do it today – send the extra money when you can afford it. It is likely a credit card of some kind and they will take whatever you send them and post it on your account. Once a month, or five times, it doesn't matter to them. You're the customer – you call the shots. Besides, it is the smartest way to avoid late charges and likely rate increases should the payment ever be late.

Here is what happens when making that effort on an imaginary $2,500 credit card with a 19 percent rate and two and a half percent minimum payments:

Making the 2.5% payments	Interest that month	Principal that month	New Balance
$62.50	$39.58	$22.92	$2,477
$61.93	$39.22	$22.71	$2,454
$61.36	$38.86	$22.50	$2,431
skipping forward to the 24th month:			
$50.57	$32.03	$18.54	$2,004

Your monthly payment will always be rounded off, but two full years and the balance is reduced by less than $500 with the minimum payments. In total, it will take 263 months (that's close to 22 years) and $3,865 in interest. Now if this payment changes to a fixed amount, where even just the first payment of $62.50 stays the same each month, it becomes:

Making the $62.50 payments	Interest that month	Principal that month	New Balance
$62.50	$39.58	$22.92	$2,477
$62.50	$39.22	$23.28	$2,454
$62.50	$38.85	$23.65	$2,430
skipping forward to the 24th month:			
$62.50	$29.61	$32.89	$1,837

Now the interest is down to $1,492 and it's done in 64 months. While it is still a lot, this is less than a quarter of the time and a lot less interest. A full chart showing these calculations, as well as the power of small extra payments, is at the end of the book.

Could you afford to add even an extra $20 to this each month? That will now make it an $82.50 fixed payment and the amount toward the principal is faster and greater. It reduces the payback to 42 months and $932 in interest. Twenty bucks and fixed payments have cut more than 18 years off the time and saved you almost $3,000 in interest. A huge difference for very little effort.

Pick the right bill – this doesn't have to be a credit card. It can be a furniture loan, or even an overdraft that is so convenient, and has been on your checking account forever. It's just that this convenience can cost you around 20 percent interest when you use it.

• It's your call and your pick – just don't kid yourself. If you're not being honest with yourself nobody else will do it for you. Since nobody else has to pay these bills, others will never care as much as you do!

 Sad but true, most people don't change until the pain level is high enough.

- Keep it in front of you – put the last statement on the fridge, or tape it to the door. It needs to always be in your face or it is out of sight – out of mind. You want it as a constant reminder. And every time you put any payment toward it, just write it on the statement with a pen and you will actually see some progress.

Slowly but surely, as you're no longer using this account, your statement will start looking a little weird. Instead of charges, you will have a whole lot of lines showing credits and payments, and it will feel great.

Then one day - the balance will be paid off. Perhaps, if you have chosen the lowest one, it might only be a matter of months. Hey, however long it takes keep asking yourself is it worth it? You bet it is.

It's OK to dream a little of what life will be like when these bills are gone for good. What will your stress level be like? What will you be able to save for that you really want, if the hangover of these bills were not around any more? Freedom is more than just being able to move around, and this REAL financial freedom is just around the corner.

When the first bill is paid off, you can move on to the next. Let's assume you've found $100 in savings when you did your budget, and now have a clear sense of your spending habits. Maybe you've changed the number of dinners out, started being aware of money leaking out each day, or perhaps just started to stretch out the length of time between dry cleaners, haircuts or other discretionary spending. Just taking this $100 and adding it to your current payments can create some incredible savings.

You'll always find a home for that last $100. Question is: will it be spent, or go to savings or debt payments?

Step-up debt repayment plan example:
1st bill: Department store card with $800 balance at 21.9%
Your minimum payment at three percent is $24, plus you are adding the $100 budget savings, so you will now be able to pay $124 each month.
Was going to take: 127 months and $920 interest
Now paid off: in 7 months and $59 total interest
Then tackle the next one:

2nd bill: Credit card with $2,000 balance at 19%
The minimum payment at three percent is $60 that you have been paying anyway, while focusing on your first bill. That payment has taken the balance down to $1,810 over those seven months at $212 interest. So now you can take the $124 you were paying on the old department store card and add it to the $60 you've been paying here all along, for a total of $184.
Was going to take: 174 months and $2,007 interest
Now paid off: in another 11 months and $385 total interest

3rd bill: Another credit card with $2,400 balance at 19%
On this balance, the minimum payment at three percent is $72, which you've paid for the time while you targeting your first two bills. Now it's time to focus on this bill in a serious way. Again, you're adding the $184 from the first two bills on top of the $72 you've been paying, for a total of $256. As you're getting focused on this one, you've already paid that $72 for 18 months, so the balance is now $1,856 and has cost $608 in interest. But that's all about to end for this card as well.
Was going to take: 187 months and $2,454 interest
Now paid off: in another 8 months and $739 total interest
You should now already be seeing how quickly extra payments

add up. And don't forget – you've only added $100 to these payments since the rest is just from interest and savings by paying everybody but yourself – and it gets even better.

4th bill: Vehicle financed (student loan or other fixed loan) of $20,000 at 7%

Hurray – the last target in our example with a payment of $396. This could be your financed or leased vehicle or any other loan. While focusing on the high interest accounts for 26 months, you've reduced this balance to $12,182 and have paid $2,478 in interest already. Now you're adding the $396 payment to the $256 from the other bills, for a total of $652.

Was going to take: 60 months and $3,763 interest
Now paid off: in another 20 months and $3,238 total interest.

The end result? You had $25,200 in debt – and were on track to pay for 15 years at a cost of more than $9,000 interest. It has taken you 46 months – less than four years – and you've saved over $4,700 interest. What has it cost you? A hundred bucks a month and a little determination!

Yes, you might get a little side tracked for a month or so, but that shouldn't discourage you. It might be hard at the start, but you will quickly become a believer when you see these bills no longer showing up in the mail. Your game plan will be different, but just as powerful and satisfying, and with the same results and huge interest savings. Following this model can become a powerful and sure-fire road map for financial success.

But it gets even better if you want. By now you have taught yourself to take charge of your money instead of giving control to all your lenders and credit card companies. You have $652 that you were paying to everybody but yourself for the last four years. If you haven't been putting some additional savings aside, maybe this is the perfect time to start. Actually it won't be hard at all since you have the $652 available with no excuses and even better – no more bills to pay.

You saw what four years accomplished by paying others. As you will read in the next chapter: Isn't it time to pay yourself first? This $652 each month, even at 8.5 percent, will now grow to over $38,000. That will be your money and not paid to any creditors. From over $25,000 in bills to debt-free in less than four years and that same length of time again to create $38,000 in savings. What a difference - and it all started with a $100 off your budget each month.

This is also the time to learn and understand the huge power of a very simple formula that you have to know to become financially successful. It is the Rule of 72, and it is very easy to remember, and the key to your financial success after debt. It calculates the length of time for your investments or savings to double, when you take the interest rate and divide it by 72. For the previous example of an 8.5 percent rate, 72 divided by 8.5 means your money will double in just over eight years without adding any more funds. Now have a look at your three percent savings and realize it will take 24 years to double, while a return of 12 percent will double every six years, and start asking some questions.

Two other points to keep in mind are:

- Don't go backwards – cancel the paid-out accounts, reduce the credit limit, instruct them to discontinue allowing cash advances (see credit card chapter for the how-to) and do whatever it takes not to have to go through this stress again.

- Can you transfer things around? Do you have a line of credit, which can be used to pay down a credit card that you've picked? It shuffles your debt around but may move it from the 17 or 19 percent range down to around half. After all, reducing your interest is the same as saving money.

 Don't cash IRAs to pay off debt. It jeopardizes your retirement savings and will be fully taxable when redeemed.

If you are able to move your debt to a lower rate, here is an example of what can happen with just a $2,000 balance at 18 percent, versus a line of credit at eight percent:

	Credit card paying the minimum	Credit card paying fixed payment	Line of credit paying the minimum	Line of credit paying fixed payment
1st Payment	$40.00		$40.00	
Time to pay	370 months		165 months	
Interest total	$4,931		$860	
Fixed payments		$40.00		$40.00
Time to pay		94 months		62 months
Interest total		$1,724		$441

From here on, always ask yourself first whether you are using credit for something that is appreciating (increasing) in value or depreciating (stereo, furniture, etc.) or whether it is a consumable (such as a meal).

Even a smart debt can quickly turn dumb. A $3,000 charge on your credit card can be smart if it is paid off in a month or so. If so, the $3,000 debt has cost you around $50 in interest – fair enough. If you choose to make the minimum payments of two percent each month, this $3,000 can now turn to a 44-year loan and cost you $9,997 in total! Even with three-percent minimum payments it is almost 17 years and $3,124 in interest.

 Make sure your credit charges are not trading a good today for a bad tomorrow.

Bad Debt Traps

The definition of debt insanity is doing the same thing you've always done and expecting different results in the future – it won't happen. You will have to do some different things to have different results. Throughout this book were many tips, tools and tricks to reduce your interest, or to borrow smarter, and shortcuts to saving interest. Here are some of the potential problem areas again:

1. Close but not all – paying close to the full balance on a credit card, but not the full statement balance. It means interest is charged on the full amount again next month – not the lower balance after you've paid a lump sum.

2. Not reducing the term on any borrowing by even just a few months when you could afford a slightly higher payment.

3. Hurray! A credit card limit increase. More temptation for little reason, and less opportunity to pay off the monthly statement if you ever do charge anywhere near the limit.

4. Carrying more than one or two cards. Quantity is not the solution, as it just spreads the debts around. It generates interest profit for more lenders, while often causing you to lose track of what the totals really add up to.

5. Not having a low interest credit card when you KNOW you're going to carry a balance each month.

6. Cash advances from credit cards.

7. No payment for X months. Delaying the start of payments also delays the final payment, adds extra interest, and is often done without a good reason.

8. Making minimum payments only, or paying late on a credit card which will trigger late charges, a likely rate increase and potential over limit charges.

9. Considering only the price of something versus the total payback of what it will cost when all is said and done.

10. Choosing poor priorities by not paying the highest interest debt first, no matter what the balance.

11. Seven year car loans (or five year and a balloon payment) and longer-term leases.

12. Any financing longer than the reasonable or useful life of the purchase (i.e. two year vacation loan).

13. Not wanting to say "I can't afford it" to others or yourself.

14. Kidding yourself in the difference between *gotta have* and *wanna have* – sales and good deals are like trains – there will always be another one along very soon.

15. Forgetting or ignoring that every time a credit card is used, line of credit accessed, or loan is signed that today's gain is always tomorrow's pain. What you're doing today will cost you something else you won't be able to do down the road.

16. Debt without something tangible: A car in the driveway with payments is quite different than a credit card balance with nothing left to show for it.

17. Feeling fortunate just to be approved instead of taking control, shopping around and asking questions to borrow your way and on your terms.

18. Knowing better and doing it anyway.

19. Just this one time, it will be OK if I charge...

20. Shopping around and actually buying on the same day when it's something expensive.

21. Starting any loan application without knowing your FICO score and its affect on your interest rate.

22. Treating credit as a substitute for income. It isn't and never will be.

23. Shopping based on payments alone.

24. To settle for a subprime interest rate without a valid reason or extensive comparison shopping.

Chapter 12

SMART: Life after Debt

 To be financially successful you just need to do some things others won't do.

There are many different kinds of smart. The first one you've been reading and learning about throughout this book. By now you have found a number of tips and ways to save you money in concrete and measurable ways. Perhaps your SMART means *Strong Motivation And The Right Tools* to turn things around. Part of that is also to continue asking the right questions – sometimes the hard questions, whether it comes to your current debt, or any new borrowing.

One of the most popular savings tools continues to be IRAs and 401(k) plans. These retirement savings contributions should be an integral part of your savings strategy, and an excellent tool for reducing your taxes. Contributions can create a tax deduction, and the interest earned within these plans keeps growing tax-free. Unlike other savings, this interest is sheltered from tax as long as it remains in the plan. It also creates a tax deduction in the year of the contribution as a nonrefundable tax credit. If you earned $25,000, you had taxes deducted on this amount throughout the year. Because of your retirement savings contribution, you will now have a tax refund, assuming there is nothing else which increases the income on your return.

Keep in mind that this refund is not free money. All it is doing is giving you back your own money. If, for example, you have invested $2,000 for retirement savings, this amount will grow over the years. With just an eight-percent return over 20 years this amount will grow to almost $10,000 without doing anything else. What a great win-win. Savings for yourself, paying less tax, and getting a refund. Now if you were to do this each year for 20 years, this investment would grow to more than $104,000. Until you reach the day of being debt-free, one of the smartest things to do with any tax refund is to sign the back of the check and pay down one of your credit cards to save even more interest. THAT is a great example of financial smarts – from beginning to end.

Another SMART acronym stands for *Saving Money And Reducing Taxes*. Saving money also includes borrowing smarter, perhaps borrowing less, or just less frequently. It also allows you to become debt-free much sooner than would otherwise be possible. The other part – saving taxes, is simply another piece of your overall finance, debt and savings plan. It is another integral part of your financial jigsaw puzzle that will save – and make you money.

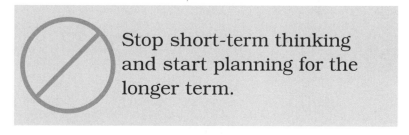

Stop short-term thinking and start planning for the longer term.

SMART is actually an acronym of Primerica Financial Services and may be another piece of putting together the puzzle of your financial health. Their mission statement includes being "in the business of changing people's lives by helping families become debt-free." It encompasses their strong desire to teach and empower clients to make better-informed decisions with a knowledge how money, credit, insurance and investments work. What a perfect ending to this book, or maybe a perfect beginning for you.

As a division of Citigroup, Primerica is part of a 1.4 trillion-dollar corporation, and one of the fastest growing companies in the financial service field. While size matters a lot, each office is an independent financial services operation with a complete range of services from mutual funds to insurance and mortgage options. Where Primerica excels head and shoulders above others is their personal dedication and service, one client at a time. What sets them apart is the training, belief and actions that the client comes first, on their terms, with their priorities, and each with unique financial means and priorities. Or as they refer to it: "Solving the fundamental problems that keep families from reaching their goals and living their dreams."

Quite a difference from being pitched – to being helped in concrete and meaningful ways. While they don't say it – it clearly shows that each of their more than 110,000 licensed representatives know they will only succeed when you do. They are there whether your goal is to gain an understanding of investment and insurance options, becoming debt-free, or starting a focused savings game plan – something big, or often quite small. It is refreshing to see a firm that talks AND practices putting the customer first. After all, wouldn't we all rather deal with someone that speaks our language, uses words and explanations we can understand, and has probably been in our situation with similar challenges?

 Want some ideas and feedback? Primerica never charges for their Financial Needs Analysis.

One of the unique features of Primerica's review of your financial situation, challenges and goals is their Financial Needs Analysis. It is designed to walk you through specific financial, debt, insurance and savings steps to determine your needs, status and goals. This powerful program is something most other companies charge hundreds of dollars for. It will also include a challenge to find your personal debt freedom date. It will be setting an actual month and year when you will be debt-free. With Primerica, there is no a charge to help families find a starting point of understanding their financial situation. Another excellent tool is their 45-page booklet *How Money Works,* which is available from most of their offices. Portions of their materials are even used in economic and business courses from high schools to universities – so there has to be something to it.

No matter what approach you choose, or what you choose to focus on, there are some important factors to consider:

• Have a proper game plan. It warrants pointing out again and again that a game plan must be both written and specific. That is why having a budget, or financial reality check, is an important step in the process of becoming debt-free. Is it helpful to ask for directions when you're lost in a strange city? You bet – but is it not more important to know where you are right now? Directions without knowing where you are won't help. The same holds true for any game plan without first understanding your current situation.

• Learn to take charge of your money. It involves hard work and dedication to get back into the driver's seat. Turn your financial situation around so you control your money instead of your bills controlling you.

 Savings prepare you for an emergency while investments help to achieve your long-term goals. Both are an invaluable part of your financial picture.

• Invest and deal with a professional manager. A well-managed portfolio goes hand in hand with an investment relationship with someone that cares. It should be a person with whom you are comfortable and someone that you trust to give you options and not a sales pitch. Only then will you allow them to hold you accountable on your shared goals, allow them to ask the right questions, and make your savings strategy a reality.

• Start to pay yourself first. Granted, this won't be easy. But when did you become less important than your bills? When did savings become a dream instead of a necessity? Do you remember your last raise? While it may not have changed your net pay much after more taxes were deducted, chances are you have now adjusted to that increased pay haven't you? Are you still barely making it at the end of the month? So where did this extra money go? What if that money had just been taken right off your check and you had never seen it, would you really have missed it? That's what it's like when you adopt the habit of paying yourself first. It is a difficult first step, but it will be worth it and just like the example above, you will be able to do it without much adjustment. To start, take your savings account off your bankcard access. It prevents you from using it without a plan, and could also save you a lot of service charges.

 Your savings should be in a place where they can't be accessed quickly—just in case you have the urge ...

To help you to start saving, one organization makes a powerful difference on a local, State and national level. It is the America Saves program managed by the Consumer Federation of America. This program is designed to encourage and help people to start saving again. Launched in Cleveland, it already has thousands of success stories and more than 20,000 people enrolled throughout the country with the help of more than 1,000 non-profit groups. Assisted by government, businesses and non-profit organizations, one of the instrumental groups behind its launch and continued success, is the excellent work, funding and leadership provided by the Ford Foundation.

Another major supporter is the National Credit Union Foundation whose member credit unions are the main financial institutions offering low or no balance accounts to encourage savings without large fees and service charges. The contact information for America Saves is in the contact section in the back of the book.

A further valuable source of information is through a credit-counseling agency, whose contact information is at the end of the book. These are professionals that will review your financial situation in strict confidence and without obligation. There is never any shame in asking for help – ever. A credit counselor can always recommend a number of alternatives for any unique debt situation and can assist with:

• Arranging repayment schedules and terms that consumers can afford, and that creditors (usually) accept.

• Developing a budget strategy that is practical and effective.

• Supplying overall credit counseling on management of debt and personal finances.

• Assisting with dispute resolution involving creditors.

• Consulting and advising on (but not handling) bankruptcy procedures when necessary.

 It is always important to do your due diligence and ask the right questions before dealing with any company.

Just make sure that you are contacting a reputable credit-counseling agency, which is a member of the National Foundation for Credit Counseling (NFCC). Many so called "new generation" counseling agencies often use commissioned salespeople to channel consumers only into debt management plans. It won't always benefit the client and can often harm their customers with improper advice, excessive fees and deceptive practices. The Credit Counseling Service of Atlanta has a partial list of excellent questions to ask when choosing a credit-counseling agency. These include:

- What is your cost? Be aware of agencies requiring a large up front fee. You should receive free budget counseling and any ongoing monthly charge or contribution should be less than 10 percent of the total debt. In fact, the Consumer Credit Counseling Service actually helps over two thirds of consumers handle challenges on their own.

- Is the company accredited? Accreditation signifies that full checks and balances are in place to protect consumers.

- How do they serve consumers? Careful as many newcomers are strictly telephone and Internet businesses with no offices or face to face counseling available.

- How is it funded? Reputable Consumer Credit Counseling agencies receive voluntary contributions from creditors who participate in Debt Management Plans, in addition to grants from the United Way, corporations and/or governments.

- Do they offer financial literacy and education programs? All NFCC member agencies have a huge commitment to helping their communities and local clients through teaching and promoting sound credit and money management practices.

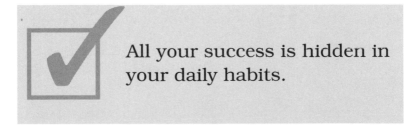

All your success is hidden in your daily habits.

A final way to become smarter is to continue to educate yourself, as knowledge really is power. Reading this book is a big step, so take full credit for it. Learning more of what works and finding available resources can also mean attending a debt counseling session. It might be a trip to the library, just doing your homework before making your next large purchase, or a range of other options. You just need to look for them, as it is often just a matter of asking the right questions.

Through these and other ways, many people find assistance or a financial coach. It all starts with you, what you want to accomplish, and where you wish to be some years from now. In the words of one of Primerica's founders, Art Williams: "You must develop a winning attitude." This means staying motivated for as long as it takes to have what you want. So sometime tonight, take a few minutes away from interruptions if you're single. If you are in a relationship, spend some time talking about what life will be like when you're debt-free. You first have to see the goal. Not what it could or might be like - stay focused and say what it WILL be like. What are your financial dreams or goals that you've never even thought possible?

I know you will make it happen and continue to use some of the tools to get smarter about credit, and to get rid of your debts sooner. To assist you further, there are also many additional tools, updates, calculators and resources available on a Web-site designed specifically for you through: www.yourmoneybook.com

To your financial success!

George J. Boelcke, F.C.I
Suite 1183 - 14781 Memorial Dr.
Houston, TX 77079
E-mail: sales@yourmoneybook.com
Web site: www.yourmoneybook.com

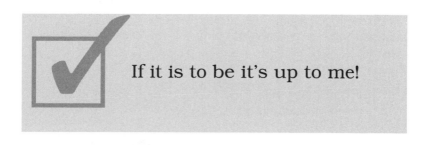

If it is to be it's up to me!

Definitions

Adjustable rate mortgage (ARM): A mortgage loan where interest rates will change with the movement of interest rates based on an index, but usually to certain maximum limits established through caps. (See also: variable interest rates)

Adverse action letter: Known as a rejection letter, and is required by law to be sent to an applicant who is turned down for credit outlining the reasons and the contact information for the credit bureau whose report was a part of the decision.

Appraised value: The value of the house (or other items) which is being used as collateral for a loan or mortgage, and done by a professional to give an unbiased value on the item or property.

Asset: What you own or can call upon, such as bonds, stock, coin collections, your vehicle, house, furniture, computer, etc.

ATM card: A plastic debit card usable in automatic teller machines (ATM machines).

APR: Annual percentage rate - the interest rate stated on an annual basis.

Balloon payment: The outstanding unpaid amount owing at a specific point in the future, usually the lump sum required to be paid at the end of a term.

Base loan rate: The lowest rate on which loans are calculated. Often based on prime, federal funds rate or treasury bill base.

Buyout: The optional purchase amount, or balance, owing on a lease at the end of the term.

Capitalized cost: Leasing jargon for the price of the vehicle.

Caps: The largest amount a variable rate mortgage can increase per year (or the entire term for lifetime caps).

Collateral: Any item(s) of security pledged against repayment.

Conditional sales contract: A sales finance agreement against a particular item pledged for security against a regular repayment plan.

Conventional mortgage: Generally the term for fixed rate 30-year mortgages which are not insured by the FHA or Veterans Administration.

Credit limit: The maximum (highest) amount that can be owed or outstanding on an account.

Credit scoring: A system of mathematical probabilities assigned to a credit application to determine the likeliness of future repayment or collection problems.

Debt ratio: See TDSR

Down payment: The money paid up front to reduce the amount to be financed.

Equity: The difference when the value of something is deducted from what is owed against the asset.

Fair Credit Reporting Act: The consumer protection laws which outline the rights of individuals with respect to credit bureaus, scoring, identity theft, access to reports and more.

First mortgage: The loan against a house, which has first claim (lien) to the property in the event of default.

Fixed rate: A charged rate of interest that does not change during the entire duration of the loan or mortgage.

Floating rate: When the interest rate charged on the loan or mortgage is adjustable (see variable rate).

Grace period: The interest-free period for credit card charges made in the current month.

Gross Debt Service: GDS is the percentage of income per year before tax, which is needed to cover payments for housing. This includes mortgage payments, taxes and homeowner association dues, where applicable.

Housing ratio: The (general) maximum amount of gross income (before tax) allowed toward housing costs per month.

Installment loan: A sum advanced in exchange for fixed regular payments, normally paid on a monthly payment basis.

Interest: The amount charged by lenders for the use of their money, which is included in the repayment terms.

Liability: What you owe – your debts.

Loan to Value ratio: The amount of mortgage compared to the value of the property expressed as a percentage.

Marginal tax rate: The rate of tax on the last $100 of income. Income tax percentages progressively increase with earnings. This calculates the tax rate on the last (highest) amount.

Maturity date: The date the loan or mortgage is due. In cases of loans, it will generally be the date the debt is paid in full.

Mortgage: A loan against real property such as a house, condo or land, which then becomes the security of the loan.

Mortgage broker: A specialist in mortgages whose primary function is to bring together the borrower with the lender. They are often ex-bankers or realtors and are compensated by a fee.

Mortgagee: The lender of a mortgage.

Mortgage refinance: To pay off an existing loan with a new one – generally to obtain a lower rate or payment, to consolidate debts or to get cash out of the equity.

OAC: On Approved Credit. The fine print of ads making credit offers that will only apply if someone is actually approved.

Overdraft: The amount by which a withdrawal brings the balance of an account below zero on any account.

PITI: Principal, interest, taxes and insurance.

Prepayment privileges: The options in a mortgage showing how much extra can be paid over and above regular payments, and at what times during the term.

Principal balance: The outstanding dollar amount of the debt.

Prime rate: The interest rate advertised and charged to the most creditworthy customers, or the base rate to which lenders will add a percentage for risk and/or their profit.

Residual: The optional purchase amount, or balance, owing on a lease at the end of the term – generally called the buyout.

Second mortgage: A further mortgage on a property when one already exists, which takes second priority after the first mortgage in the event of default and/or foreclosure.

Secured loan: A loan guaranteed by security of assets pledged against repayment.

Security: See collateral

TDSR: Total Debt Service Ratio. The percentage of total income allowed toward all bills and monthly payments, generally restricted to 36 or 38 percent.

Term: The period of time during which a loan is set up for and (generally) repaid in full.

Unsecured loan: A loan obtained without pledging security or assets from the borrower, also known as a note loan.

Variable rate: A rate of interest subject to change during the term of a loan or mortgage based on a pre-agreed formula.

Variable rate mortgage: A mortgage where the interest rate changes with market conditions, generally monthly, twice a year or annually. Mortgage payments remain the same for a period of time, but the amount that is applied to principal will vary as the interest amount will come out of the total payment first.

Statement of Assets & Liabilities

Assets		Liabilities	
Cash and savings	$_____	Car loan(s)	$_____
Value of current home	$_____	Bank loan(s)	$_____
Other real estate owned	$_____	Current mortgage	$_____
Stocks or bonds	$_____	Other mortgage	$_____
Cash value		Credit card balances	
of life insurance	$_____	a)_____	$_____
Automobile(s)	$_____	b)_____	$_____
	$_____	c)_____	$_____
Other assets (detail)		d)_____	$_____
_____	$_____	Other loans or debts	
_____	$_____	_____	$_____
_____	$_____	_____	$_____
Total assets:	$_____	**Total liabilities:**	$_____

Total assets minus total liabilities = Net worth: $_____

Debt Service & Income Worksheet

Gross monthly income (before tax) $_____

Spouse monthly income (before tax) $_____

Other income (verifiable) $_____
   Including alimony, child support, etc.

Total Gross income: $_____(a)

Multiply times 0.28 for maximum
   monthly mortgage payment/tax & insurance $_____(b)

Multiply time 0.33 for maximum
   monthly jumbo loan payment $_____(c)

Multiply times 0.36 for maximum
 total debt load you can carry per month $_____(d)

Debt Load Calculation

Current monthly payments

Car loan(s) $_____

Credit card(s) minimum payment(s) $_____

Other installment plan payment(s) $_____

Other payment $_____

Total current monthly payments $_____(e)

Available for payments:

(a) gross income minus (e) current payments is the maximum payment *room* for <u>any new borrowing</u>:$_____(f)

The <u>lower</u> figure of (b) which is 28% of your gross income,

or (f) which is the maximum for any new borrowing is the <u>highest mortgage payment</u> you can qualify for:$_____

MONTHLY SPENDING

	How much spent each month:	Could you lower it by:
HOUSING		
Mortgage or rent		
Property tax		
Water/sewer/trash		
Gas		
Electricity		
Telephone		
Phone/cell & internet		
Cable & satellite		
Home repairs/maintenance		
VEHICLES & TRANSPORT		
Loan or lease payment		
Repairs/maintenance		
Parking		
Gas/oil		
Bus/train/subway/tolls		
FOOD		
Groceries		
Meals out		
Lunch at work		
CLOTHING		
Adults		
Kid(s)		
KID'S EXPENSES		
School fees & charges		
Daycare		
Allowance		
Sports & other activities		
School lunches		
Child support payments		

MONTHLY SPENDING (Continued)

	How much spent each month:	Could you lower it by:

CURRENT PAYMENTS

Credit card _____ _____
Credit card _____ _____
Credit card _____ _____
Student loan _____ _____
Credit line _____ _____

PERSONAL EXPENSES

Memberships _____ _____
Dues & subscriptions _____ _____
Presents/donations _____ _____
Personal spending money _____ _____
Hairdresser/drycleaning _____ _____
Hobbies _____ _____

PAYING YOURSELF

RRSP monthly savings _____ _____
Other savings plan _____ _____

INSURANCE

Vehicle _____ _____
House or content _____ _____
Life _____ _____
Disability _____ _____

MEDICAL

Prescriptions _____ _____
Dental/Eye care _____ _____
Healthcare premiums _____ _____
Drugs/vitamins _____ _____

ENTERTAINMENT

Sports & recreation _____ _____

GRAND TOTAL: $:_____ $:_____

TOTAL SPENT EACH MONTH   TOTAL POSSIBLE SAVINGS

Resources and Contact Information

Federal Agencies Complaints:

Comptroller of the Currency
Compliance Management
250 E Street NW
Washington, DC 20019
800 613 6742

Federal Deposit Insurance Corporation
Division of Compliance & Consumer Affairs
550-17 Street NW
Washington, DC 20429
202 898 3536

Federal Reserve
Consumer & Community Affairs
20 Street & Constitution Avenue
Washington, DC 20551
202 452 3693
Web site: bog.frb.fed.us

The Federal Trade Commission
Credit Practices Division
Washington, DC 20580
202 326 3128
877 382 4357
Web site: ftc.gov
The FTC works for consumers to prevent deceptive, fraudulent or unfair business practices and providing consumer information.

National Credit Union Administration
1775 Duke Street
Alexandria, VA 22314
703 518 6330

Office of Thrift Supervision
Consumer Affairs Division
1700 G Street NW
Washington, DC 20552
800 842 6929

With overlapping jurisdictions, large bureaucracies, specific mandates and a range of federal regulations, it is often hard to tell which agency to contact. All these agencies are required to forward any concerns or complaints to the appropriate agency. If you are in doubt, start with the most powerful one, which is the Federal Reserve.

Other Resources and Contacts:

American Bankers Association
120 Connecticut Avenue NW
Washington, DC 20036
202 663 5000

The ABA is the voice of the banking industry. It is a member organization, which provides education, communication, training and research to the banking industry.

America Saves
Consumer Federation of America Foundation
1424-16 St. NW
Washington, DC 20036
202 387 6121
Web site: americasaves.org

This is a national campaign to encourage people to save and build wealth. America Saves is managed by the non-profit Consumer Federation of America, as discussed in Chapter 12.

Council of Better Business Bureaus (BBB)
800-4200 Wilson Boulevard
Arlington, Virginia 22203
703 276 0100

This is the umbrella organization for all local BBBs who act as a pro-active consumer ally. Your local and State offices will be in the telephone directory.

Debtors Anonymous
Box 920888
Needham, MA 02492-0009
781 453 2743
Web site: debtorsanonymous.org

Debtors Anonymous is a nonprofit organization, which serves as a resource through its policy of cooperation but not affiliating with the professional community. A listing of meetings in various States is available on their Web site or by telephone.

Genworth Financial
6620 W. Broad Street
Richmond, VA 23230
888 436 9678
Web site: www.genworth.com

One of the largest financial services firms in the world and a leader in providing mortgage insurance with over 15 million clients and growing. Their Web site has a list and link to lenders who offers their mortgage insurance in all 50 States through www.gehomenow.com, as well as excellent resources, tools and tips for home buyers.

Institute of Certified Financial Planners
301-7600 East Eastman Avenue
Denver, CO 80231-4397

The member association to obtain a list of certified financial planners in your State, plus other selection information.

Primerica Financial Services

Each office is independently owned and managed, and thousands of offices are located throughout the country, in every State, and almost every community. Their contact information is available through your local telephone directory.

Web site: www.primerica.com

Leasing Concerns or Inquiries:

Federal Reserve Board
Division of Consumer & Community Affairs
Mail Stop 800
Washington, DC 20551 or:

Federal Trade Commission
Consumer Response Center
6th and Pennsylvania Avenue, NW
Washington, DC 20580

The federal Consumer Leasing Act as well as some State laws may have additional consumer rights, which may not be shown in your lease. To obtain further information, contact you State's consumer protection agency, or attorney general's office which are found in the telephone directory, or contact the above offices directly.

Consumer Credit Counseling Contacts

The National Foundation for Credit Counseling (NFCC), through its member agencies sets the national standards for quality credit counseling, debt reduction services and education. The NFCC, with more than 1,000 community based offices assists more than 1.5 million families each year.

National Foundation for Credit Counseling (NFCC)
900-801 Roeder Rd.
Silver Spring, MD 20910
Telephone: 301 589 5600

To find an NFCC member location:
• Call 800 388 2227 with 24-hour automated assistance for all States.
• Or through their member agency locator at: www.nfcc.org

Opting Out of Credit Card Solicitations

To stop credit card solicitations by mail or phone contact the following organizations:

• Call 1 888 5 OPTOUT (1 888 567 8688) to request removal of your name from direct marketing lists. You will supply some basic identification information for a five year block of credit offers which have prescreened your file.

• Contact the individual credit bureaus to opt out of pre-approval screening inquiries of your credit file:

> Equifax Inc. Marketing Opt-Out
> Box 740123
> Atlanta, GA 30374-0123
> Phone: 800 556 4711

> Experian Marketing Opt-Out
> Box 919
> Allen, TX 75013
> Phone: 800 353 0809

> TransUnion Marketing Opt-Out
> Box 97328
> Jackson, MS 39288-7328
> Phone: 800 680 7293

• Register your telephone number(s) with the National Do Not Call Registry (www.donotcall.gov) administered by the Federal Trade Commission and enforced as of October 1, 2003. To register a residential or cell phone number or to confirm that your number is on the National Registry call: 888 382 1222 (You must call from the phone number you are wishing to register).

• Write to the Direct Marketing Association to also opt out of any pre-approved offers. You will need to supply your full name, current address and telephone number.

> Direct Marketing Association
> Attn: Mail Preference Service
> Box 1559
> Carmel, NY 10512

Major Credit Card Companies:

American Express
Public Relations Department
American Express Tower, World Financial Center
200 Vessey Street
New York, NY 10285
212 640 2000
Web site: www.americanexpress.com

Discover Card
Public Relations Department
2500 Lakecook Road
Riverwoods, Il 60015
800 347 2683
Web site: www.discovercard.com

MasterCard International
Public Relations Department
888 – 7th Avenue
New York, NY 10106
800 999 5136
Web site: mastercard.com

Visa USA
Public Relations Department
Box 8999
San Francisco, CA 94128-8999
800 8472511
Web site: www.visa.com

Credit Union Locator

Credit Union National Association
Box 431
Madison, WI 53701-0431
800 356 9655
Web site: www.cuna.org

State Credit Union Contacts & Information:

Alabama Credit Union League   205 991 9710
Web site: www.acul.com

Alaska Credit Union League   907 562 1255
Web site: www.alaskacreditunions.org

Arkansas Credit Union League   501 376 6508
Web site: www.acul.org

Arizona Credit Union System   602 264 6701
Web site: azcreditunions.coop

California Credit Union League   800 472 1702
Web site: www.ccul.org

Colorado Credit Union System   303 427 4222
Web site: colocu.com

Connecticut Credit Union Association   203 265 5657
Web site: ctcua.org

D.C. Credit Union League   703 836 9092
Web site: vacul.org

Delaware Credit Union League   302 322 9341
Web site: dcul.org

Florida Credit Union League   850 576 8171
Web site: fcul.org

Georgia Credit Union Affiliates   800 768 4282
Web site: gcua.org

Hawaii Credit Union League   809 941 0556
Web site: hcul.org

Iowa Credit Union League   515 226 9999
Web site: ia-icul.org

Idaho Credit Union League   208 343 4841
Web site: idahocul.org

Illinois Credit Union System   630 983 3400
Web site: iculeague.coop

Indiana Credit Union League   317 594 5300
Web site: icul.org

Kansas Credit Union Association   316 206 2203
Web site: kcua.org

Kentucky Credit Union League   502 459 8023
Web site: kycul.org

Louisiana Credit Union League   504 736 3650
Web site: lcul.com

Massachusetts CU League   508 481 6755
Web site: cucenter.org/ma

Maryland Credit Union League   410 290 6858
Web site: mdcul.org

Maine Credit Union League   207 773 5671
Web site: mainecul.org

Michigan Credit Union League   734 420 1530
Web site: mcul..com

Minnesota Credit Union Network   952 854 3071
Web site: mncun.org

Missouri Credit Union Association   314 542 0555
Web site: mcua.org

Mississippi Credit Union Association   601 981 4552
Web site: mcus.com

Montana Credit Union Network   406 442 9081
Web site: mcun.org

North Carolina Credit Union Network   336 299 6286
Web site: ncleague.org

North Dakota Credit Union League   701 258 5760
Web site: dcu.org

Nebraska Credit Union League   402 333 9331
Web site: nebrcul.org

New Hampshire Credit Union League   508 481 6755
Web site: nhcul.org

New Jersey Credit Union League   609 448 2426
Web site: njcul.org

New Mexico (Credit Union Association of)   505 298 9899
Web site: cuanm.org

Nevada Credit Union League   909 980 8890
Web site: ccul.org

New York State Credit Union League   518 437 8100
Web site: nyscul.org

Ohio Credit Union System   614 336 2894
Web site: ohiocul.org

Oklahoma Credit Union League   918 496 4688
Web site: okleague.coop

Oregon (Credit Union Association of)   503 641 8420
Web site: cuao.org

Pennsylvania Credit Union Association   717 234 3156
Web site: pcua.coop

Rhode Island Credit Union League   508 481 6755
Web site: riculeague.org

South Carolina Credit Union League   803 781 5400
Web site: sccul.org

South Dakota Credit Union League   605 336 3155
Web site: sdcul.com

Tennessee Credit Union League   423 899 2425
Web site: yourleague.org

Texas Credit Union League   469 385 6400
Web site: tcul.coop

Utah League of Credit Unions   801 972 3400
Web site: ulcu.com

Virginia Credit Union League   434 237 9600
Web site: vacul.org

Vermont Credit Union League   802 863 7848
Web site: vermontcreditunions.com

Washington CU League   206 340 4111
Web site: waleague.org

Wisconsin Credit Union League   262 549 0200
Web site: wcul.org

West Virginia Credit Union League   304 485 4521
Web site: wvcul.org

Wyoming Credit Union League   303 427 4222
Web site: wyomingleague.coop

Credit Union Match Up Program:

Every credit union has their own membership criteria. Some serve entire communities, while other serve members of specific professions (such as teachers, fire fighters, etc.), or offer memberships to entire communities.

To be referred to a credit union in your community, contact your State's credit union league or the match up program through:

• Their Web-site at: www.acu.org
• By telephone at: 800 469 8656

Credit Bureaus Contact Information

Equifax Information Service Center
Box 740241
Atlanta, GA 30374
Consumer contact number: 800 685 1111
Report order number: 800 685 1111
Fraud alert & reporting line: 800 525 6285
Web site: www.equifax.com

Experian (formerly TRW Consumer Credit Service)
National Consumer Assistance Center
Box 2104
Allen, TX 75013
Consumer contact number: 888 397 3742
Report order number: 888 397 3742
Fraud alert & reporting line: 888 397 3742
Disputing report content: 866 200 6020
Web site: www.experian.com

TransUnion Credit Information Company
Consumer Inquiries
Box 2000
Chester, PA 19022
Consumer contact number: 800 916 8800
Report order number: 800 888 4213
Fraud alert & reporting line: 800 680 7289
Web site: www.transunion.com

Obtaining a Copy of Your Credit Report

You have the right to obtain a copy of your credit report at no charge once each year from every credit reporting agency.

To request the report, you need to do so by mail or telephone and advise the credit bureau that you are calling to obtain your free annual report. To order a report on-line you will be charge a fee. For a more frequent report, your cost will vary by state to a maximum of approximately $9.00. To also receive your FICO score with your credit report, there will be an additional charge. Or you can order your FICO score (and also your credit reports) directly from The Fair Isaac Corporation at: www.myfico.com

Free credit report Web site established by the Federal Trade Commission:

By mail: Annual Credit Report Request Service
                Box 105281
                Atlanta, GA 30348-5281
By phone: 877 322 8228
On-line: www.annualcreditreport.com

Your Rights Under the Fair Credit Reporting Act:

The following are some basic highlights:

Fraud alert: Consumers have the right to request a fraud alert on their file for 90 days. With a proper identity theft report from a law enforcement agency, this can be extended for a period of up to seven years. It also assures that this alert is included with all credit reports and credit scores. Credit grantors cannot extend credit, change limits, or issue new credit cards without contacting the consumer and taking reasonable verification steps. Credit bureaus are also obligated to share fraud alerts with each other to assure consumers can protect themselves with one telephone call. Anyone with an extended fraud alert is then entitled to two free credit reports in the first year. Extended fraud alerts are also automatically opted out of having companies pre-screening their file for five years.

Trade line blocking: This requires credit reporting agencies to block fraudulent trade reports in a file when a proper identity-theft report has been filed. This measure is designed to prevent the spread of incorrect information beyond the damage that has already been done.

Records disclosure: With a proper police report, consumers have the right to obtain copies of records and information from businesses where the identity theft occurred and establishments who opened these accounts. Businesses at that point have 30 days to supply the full documentation.

Reinvestigation: Credit reporting agencies have up to 45 days to reinvestigate items disputed by a consumer.

Credit bureaus to supply credit scores: Credit reporting agencies must also supply up to four reasons (key factors) which have adversely affected a consumer's score.

The charges for credit scores: The fee for obtaining a credit score must be fair and reasonable, as determined by the Federal Trade Commission.

Mortgage lenders must supply credit score: All mortgage lenders must supply the credit score and information on the key reasons for it to anyone who has applied with them at no charge.

Notification of negative information: Lenders who supply negative information to credit reporting agencies are required to advise consumers that this has been (or is being) done. This is designed to make consumers aware that their credit file has (or is about to be) adversely affected, partly to be pro-active and to avoid any later surprise.

Increased rates due to risk: Lenders are required to notify consumers that their terms and/or rate are based on information from their consumer credit report, and to disclose that the consumer is entitled to a free copy of their report. This applies when terms and/or rates are "materially less favorable than the most favorable terms available to a substantial portion of consumers." In other words, this disclosure applies when the rate being charged is significantly higher than the average client would be paying.

Credit Cards at 13%

Making minimum 2.5% payments
or adding $20 per month and making fixed payments

Balance	Minimum payment starts at	Months to pay in full	Total interest	Add $20 & fix payments to	Months to pay in full	Total interest now	Interest saved
$500	$13	69	$204	$33	17	$50	$154
$750	$19	97	$395	$39	22	$96	$299
$1,000	$25	117	$586	$45	26	$150	$436
$1,500	$38	146	$968	$58	31	$272	$696
$2,000	$50	166	$1,351	$70	35	$406	$945
$2,500	$63	182	$1,733	$83	37	$547	$1,186
$3,000	$75	194	$2,115	$95	39	$692	$1,423
$3,500	$88	205	$2,498	$108	41	$840	$1,658
$4,000	$100	215	$2,880	$120	42	$990	$1,890
$4,500	$113	223	$3,262	$133	43	$1,141	$2,121
$5,000	$125	230	$3,645	$145	44	$1,294	$2,351
$6,000	$150	243	$4,409	$170	45	$1,602	$2,807
$7,000	$175	254	$5,174	$195	46	$1,913	$3,261
$8,000	$200	263	$5,939	$220	47	$2,225	$3,714
$9,000	$225	271	$6,703	$245	48	$2,538	$4,165
$10,000	$250	279	$7,468	$270	49	$2,852	$4,616

Making minimum 3% payments
or adding $20 per month and making fixed payments

Balance	Minimum payment starts at	Months to pay in full	Total interest	Add $20 & fix payments to	Months to pay in full	Total interest now	Interest saved
$500	$15	63	$177	$35	16	$46	$131
$750	$23	84	$318	$43	20	$87	$231
$1,000	$30	99	$459	$50	23	$133	$326
$1,500	$45	120	$742	$65	27	$235	$507
$2,000	$60	135	$1,024	$80	30	$345	$679
$2,500	$75	146	$1,307	$95	32	$459	$848
$3,000	$90	156	$1,590	$110	33	$575	$1,015
$3,500	$105	164	$1,872	$125	34	$693	$1,179
$4,000	$120	170	$2,155	$140	35	$812	$1,343
$4,500	$135	177	$2,437	$155	36	$932	$1,505
$5,000	$150	182	$2,720	$170	36	$1,053	$1,667
$6,000	$180	191	$3,285	$200	37	$1,296	$1,989
$7,000	$210	199	$3,850	$230	38	$1,539	$2,311
$8,000	$240	206	$4,416	$260	38	$1,784	$2,632
$9,000	$270	212	$4,981	$290	39	$2,029	$2,952
$10,000	$300	218	$5,546	$320	39	$2,275	$3,271

Credit Cards at 19%

Making minimum 2.5% payments
or adding $20 per month and making fixed payments

Balance	Minimum payment starts at	Months to pay in full	Total interest	Add $20 & fix payments to	Months to pay in full	Total interest now	Interest saved
$500	$13	$89	$411	$33	$18	$78	$333
$750	$19	$133	$843	$39	$24	$153	$690
$1,000	$25	$164	$1,275	$45	$28	$242	$1,033
$1,500	$38	$208	$2,138	$58	$34	$450	$1,688
$2,000	$50	$239	$3,002	$70	$39	$683	$2,319
$2,500	$63	$263	$3,865	$83	$42	$932	$2,933
$3,000	$75	$283	$4,729	$95	$45	$1,192	$3,537
$3,500	$88	$300	$5,593	$108	$47	$1,459	$4,134
$4,000	$100	$314	$6,456	$120	$48	$1,732	$4,724
$4,500	$113	$327	$7,320	$133	$50	$2,008	$5,312
$5,000	$125	$339	$8,184	$145	$51	$2,288	$5,896
$6,000	$150	$358	$9,911	$170	$53	$2,855	$7,056
$7,000	$175	$375	$11,638	$195	$54	$3,430	$8,208
$8,000	$200	$390	$13,365	$220	$55	$4,008	$9,357
$9,000	$225	$402	$15,092	$245	$56	$4,590	$10,502
$10,000	$250	$414	$16,819	$270	$57	$5,175	$11,644

Making minimum 3% payments
or adding $20 per month and making fixed payments

Balance	Minimum payment starts at	Months to pay in full	Total interest	Add $20 & fix payments to	Months to pay in full	Total interest now	Interest saved
$500	$15	$77	$330	$35	$17	$71	$259
$750	$23	$105	$610	$43	$21	$136	$474
$1,000	$30	$125	$889	$50	$25	$212	$677
$1,500	$45	$154	$1,448	$65	$29	$382	$1,066
$2,000	$60	$174	$2,007	$80	$30	$522	$1,485
$2,500	$75	$189	$2,566	$95	$35	$760	$1,806
$3,000	$90	$202	$3,124	$110	$36	$958	$2,166
$3,500	$105	$213	$3,683	$125	$38	$1,161	$2,522
$4,000	$120	$222	$4,242	$140	$39	$1,367	$2,875
$4,500	$135	$231	$4,801	$155	$40	$1,574	$3,227
$5,000	$150	$238	$5,360	$170	$40	$1,783	$3,577
$6,000	$180	$251	$6,477	$200	$42	$2,203	$4,274
$7,000	$210	$262	$7,595	$230	$42	$2,627	$4,968
$8,000	$240	$271	$8,712	$260	$43	$3,053	$5,659
$9,000	$270	$279	$9,830	$290	$44	$3,480	$6,350
$10,000	$300	$287	$10,948	$320	$44	$3,909	$7,039

Credit Cards at 22%

Making minimum 2.5% payments
or adding $20 per month and making fixed payments

Balance	Minimum payment starts at	Months to pay in full	Total interest	Add $20 & fix payments to	Months to pay in full	Total interest now	Interest saved
$500	$13	$107	$603	$33	$19	$93	$510
$750	$19	$167	$1,290	$39	$25	$185	$1,105
$1,000	$25	$210	$1,977	$45	$29	$296	$1,681
$1,500	$38	$271	$3,352	$58	$36	$559	$2,793
$2,000	$50	$314	$4,727	$70	$41	$859	$3,868
$2,500	$63	$347	$6,102	$83	$45	$1,183	$4,919
$3,000	$75	$374	$7,477	$95	$48	$1,523	$5,954
$3,500	$88	$398	$8,852	$108	$51	$1,876	$6,976
$4,000	$100	$417	$10,227	$120	$52	$2,238	$7,989
$4,500	$113	$435	$11,602	$133	$54	$2,608	$8,994
$5,000	$125	$451	$12,977	$145	$56	$2,983	$9,994
$6,000	$150	$478	$15,727	$170	$58	$3,746	$11,981

Making minimum 3% payments
or adding $20 per month and making fixed payments

Balance	Minimum payment starts at	Months to pay in full	Total interest	Add $20 & fix payments to	Months to pay in full	Total interest now	Interest saved
$500	$15	$87	$448	$35	$17	$85	$363
$750	$23	$122	$841	$43	$22	$164	$677
$1,000	$30	$146	$1,234	$50	$26	$257	$977
$1,500	$45	$181	$2,020	$65	$31	$468	$1,552
$2,000	$60	$205	$2,806	$80	$34	$701	$2,105
$2,500	$75	$224	$3,591	$95	$37	$944	$2,647
$3,000	$90	$240	$4,377	$110	$39	$1,197	$3,180
$3,500	$105	$253	$5,163	$125	$40	$1,455	$3,708
$4,000	$120	$264	$5,948	$140	$41	$1,718	$4,230
$4,500	$135	$274	$6,734	$155	$42	$1,983	$4,751
$5,000	$150	$283	$7,520	$170	$43	$2,751	$4,769
$6,000	$180	$299	$9,091	$200	$44	$2,791	$6,300

Loan Payment Table   5.0% Rate

Term in Years	3	4	5	6	7	10	15	20	25	30
Amount										
$1,000	$30	$23	$19	$16	$14	$11	$8	$7	$6	$5
$2,000	$60	$46	$38	$32	$28	$21	$16	$13	$12	$11
$3,000	$90	$69	$57	$48	$42	$32	$24	$20	$18	$16
$4,000	$120	$92	$75	$64	$57	$42	$32	$26	$23	$21
$5,000	$150	$115	$94	$81	$71	$53	$40	$33	$29	$27
$6,000	$180	$138	$113	$97	$85	$64	$47	$40	$35	$32
$7,000	$210	$161	$132	$113	$99	$74	$55	$46	$41	$38
$8,000	$240	$184	$151	$129	$113	$85	$63	$53	$47	$43
$9,000	$270	$207	$170	$145	$127	$95	$71	$59	$53	$48
$10,000	$300	$230	$189	$161	$141	$106	$79	$66	$58	$54
$11,000	$330	$253	$208	$177	$155	$117	$87	$73	$64	$59
$12,000	$360	$276	$226	$193	$170	$127	$95	$79	$70	$64
$13,000	$390	$299	$245	$209	$184	$138	$103	$86	$76	$70
$14,000	$420	$322	$264	$225	$198	$148	$111	$92	$82	$75
$15,000	$450	$345	$283	$242	$212	$159	$119	$99	$88	$81
$16,000	$480	$368	$302	$258	$226	$170	$127	$106	$94	$86
$17,000	$510	$391	$321	$274	$240	$180	$134	$112	$99	$91
$18,000	$539	$415	$340	$290	$254	$191	$142	$119	$105	$97
$19,000	$569	$438	$359	$306	$269	$202	$150	$125	$111	$102
$20,000	$599	$461	$377	$322	$283	$212	$158	$132	$117	$107
$25,000	$749	$576	$472	$403	$353	$265	$198	$165	$146	$134
$30,000	$899	$691	$566	$483	$424	$318	$237	$198	$175	$161
$35,000	$1,049	$806	$660	$564	$495	$371	$277	$231	$205	$188
$40,000	$1,199	$921	$755	$644	$565	$424	$316	$264	$234	$215
$45,000	$1,349	$1,036	$849	$725	$636	$477	$356	$297	$263	$242
$50,000	$1,499	$1,151	$944	$805	$707	$530	$395	$330	$292	$268
$55,000	$1,648	$1,267	$1,038	$886	$777	$583	$435	$363	$322	$295
$60,000	$1,798	$1,382	$1,132	$966	$848	$636	$474	$396	$351	$322
$65,000	$1,948	$1,497	$1,227	$1,047	$919	$689	$514	$429	$380	$349
$70,000	$2,098	$1,612	$1,321	$1,127	$989	$742	$554	$462	$409	$376
$75,000	$2,248	$1,727	$1,415	$1,208	$1,060	$795	$593	$495	$438	$403
$80,000	$2,398	$1,842	$1,510	$1,288	$1,131	$849	$633	$528	$468	$429
$85,000	$2,548	$1,957	$1,604	$1,369	$1,201	$902	$672	$561	$497	$456
$90,000	$2,697	$2,073	$1,698	$1,449	$1,272	$955	$712	$594	$526	$483
$100,000	$2,997	$2,303	$1,887	$1,610	$1,413	$1,061	$791	$660	$585	$537
$125,000	$3,746	$2,879	$2,359	$2,013	$1,767	$1,326	$988	$825	$731	$671
$150,000	$4,496	$3,454	$2,831	$2,416	$2,120	$1,591	$1,186	$990	$877	$805
$175,000	$5,245	$4,030	$3,302	$2,818	$2,473	$1,856	$1,384	$1,155	$1,023	$939
$200,000	$5,994	$4,606	$3,774	$3,221	$2,827	$2,121	$1,582	$1,320	$1,169	$1,074
$225,000	$6,743	$5,182	$4,246	$3,624	$3,180	$2,386	$1,779	$1,485	$1,315	$1,208
$250,000	$7,493	$5,757	$4,718	$4,026	$3,533	$2,652	$1,977	$1,650	$1,461	$1,342
$275,000	$8,242	$6,333	$5,190	$4,429	$3,887	$2,917	$2,175	$1,815	$1,608	$1,476
$300,000	$8,991	$6,909	$5,661	$4,831	$4,240	$3,182	$2,372	$1,980	$1,754	$1,610

Loan Payment Table

5.25% Rate

Term in Years	3	4	5	6	7	10	15	20	25	30
Amount										
$1,000	$30	$23	$19	$16	$14	$11	$8	$7	$6	$6
$2,000	$60	$46	$38	$32	$29	$21	$16	$13	$12	$11
$3,000	$90	$69	$57	$49	$43	$32	$24	$20	$18	$17
$4,000	$120	$93	$76	$65	$57	$43	$32	$27	$24	$22
$5,000	$150	$116	$95	$81	$71	$54	$40	$34	$30	$28
$6,000	$180	$139	$114	$97	$86	$64	$48	$40	$36	$33
$7,000	$211	$162	$133	$114	$100	$75	$56	$47	$42	$39
$8,000	$241	$185	$152	$130	$114	$86	$64	$54	$48	$44
$9,000	$271	$208	$171	$146	$128	$97	$72	$61	$54	$50
$10,000	$301	$231	$190	$162	$143	$107	$80	$67	$60	$55
$11,000	$331	$255	$209	$178	$157	$118	$88	$74	$66	$61
$12,000	$361	$278	$228	$195	$171	$129	$96	$81	$72	$66
$13,000	$391	$301	$247	$211	$185	$139	$105	$88	$78	$72
$14,000	$421	$324	$266	$227	$200	$150	$113	$94	$84	$77
$15,000	$451	$347	$285	$243	$214	$161	$121	$101	$90	$83
$16,000	$481	$370	$304	$260	$228	$172	$129	$108	$96	$88
$17,000	$511	$393	$323	$276	$242	$182	$137	$115	$102	$94
$18,000	$541	$417	$342	$292	$257	$193	$145	$121	$108	$99
$19,000	$572	$440	$361	$308	$271	$204	$153	$128	$114	$105
$20,000	$602	$463	$380	$324	$285	$215	$161	$135	$120	$110
$25,000	$752	$579	$475	$406	$356	$268	$201	$168	$150	$138
$30,000	$902	$694	$570	$487	$428	$322	$241	$202	$180	$166
$35,000	$1,053	$810	$665	$568	$499	$376	$281	$236	$210	$193
$40,000	$1,203	$926	$759	$649	$570	$429	$322	$270	$240	$221
$45,000	$1,354	$1,041	$854	$730	$641	$483	$362	$303	$270	$248
$50,000	$1,504	$1,157	$949	$811	$713	$536	$402	$337	$300	$276
$55,000	$1,655	$1,273	$1,044	$892	$784	$590	$442	$371	$330	$304
$60,000	$1,805	$1,389	$1,139	$973	$855	$644	$482	$404	$360	$331
$65,000	$1,955	$1,504	$1,234	$1,054	$926	$697	$523	$438	$390	$359
$70,000	$2,106	$1,620	$1,329	$1,135	$998	$751	$563	$472	$419	$387
$75,000	$2,256	$1,736	$1,424	$1,217	$1,069	$805	$603	$505	$449	$414
$80,000	$2,407	$1,851	$1,519	$1,298	$1,140	$858	$643	$539	$479	$442
$85,000	$2,557	$1,967	$1,614	$1,379	$1,211	$912	$683	$573	$509	$469
$90,000	$2,707	$2,083	$1,709	$1,460	$1,283	$966	$723	$606	$539	$497
$100,000	$3,008	$2,314	$1,899	$1,622	$1,425	$1,073	$804	$674	$599	$552
$125,000	$3,760	$2,893	$2,373	$2,028	$1,781	$1,341	$1,005	$842	$749	$690
$150,000	$4,512	$3,471	$2,848	$2,433	$2,138	$1,609	$1,206	$1,011	$899	$828
$175,000	$5,265	$4,050	$3,323	$2,839	$2,494	$1,878	$1,407	$1,179	$1,049	$966
$200,000	$6,017	$4,629	$3,797	$3,244	$2,850	$2,146	$1,608	$1,348	$1,198	$1,104
$225,000	$6,769	$5,207	$4,272	$3,650	$3,207	$2,414	$1,809	$1,516	$1,348	$1,242
$250,000	$7,521	$5,786	$4,746	$4,055	$3,563	$2,682	$2,010	$1,685	$1,498	$1,381
$275,000	$8,273	$6,364	$5,221	$4,461	$3,919	$2,951	$2,211	$1,853	$1,648	$1,519
$300,000	$9,025	$6,943	$5,696	$4,866	$4,276	$3,219	$2,412	$2,022	$1,798	$1,657

Loan Payment Table   5.50% Rate

Term in Years Amount	3	4	5	6	7	10	15	20	25	30
$1,000	$30	$23	$19	$16	$14	$11	$8	$7	$6	$6
$2,000	$60	$47	$38	$33	$29	$22	$16	$14	$12	$11
$3,000	$91	$70	$57	$49	$43	$33	$25	$21	$18	$17
$4,000	$121	$93	$76	$65	$57	$43	$33	$28	$25	$23
$5,000	$151	$116	$96	$82	$72	$54	$41	$34	$31	$28
$6,000	$181	$140	$115	$98	$86	$65	$49	$41	$37	$34
$7,000	$211	$163	$134	$114	$101	$76	$57	$48	$43	$40
$8,000	$242	$186	$153	$131	$115	$87	$65	$55	$49	$45
$9,000	$272	$209	$172	$147	$129	$98	$74	$62	$55	$51
$10,000	$302	$233	$191	$163	$144	$109	$82	$69	$61	$57
$11,000	$332	$256	$210	$180	$158	$119	$90	$76	$68	$62
$12,000	$362	$279	$229	$196	$172	$130	$98	$83	$74	$68
$13,000	$393	$302	$248	$212	$187	$141	$106	$89	$80	$74
$14,000	$423	$326	$267	$229	$201	$152	$114	$96	$86	$79
$15,000	$453	$349	$287	$245	$216	$163	$123	$103	$92	$85
$16,000	$483	$372	$306	$261	$230	$174	$131	$110	$98	$91
$17,000	$513	$395	$325	$278	$244	$184	$139	$117	$104	$97
$18,000	$544	$419	$344	$294	$259	$195	$147	$124	$111	$102
$19,000	$574	$442	$363	$310	$273	$206	$155	$131	$117	$108
$20,000	$604	$465	$382	$327	$287	$217	$163	$138	$123	$114
$25,000	$755	$581	$478	$408	$359	$271	$204	$172	$154	$142
$30,000	$906	$698	$573	$490	$431	$326	$245	$206	$184	$170
$35,000	$1,057	$814	$669	$572	$503	$380	$286	$241	$215	$199
$40,000	$1,208	$930	$764	$654	$575	$434	$327	$275	$246	$227
$45,000	$1,359	$1,047	$860	$735	$647	$488	$368	$310	$276	$256
$50,000	$1,510	$1,163	$955	$817	$719	$543	$409	$344	$307	$284
$55,000	$1,661	$1,279	$1,051	$899	$790	$597	$449	$378	$338	$312
$60,000	$1,812	$1,395	$1,146	$980	$862	$651	$490	$413	$368	$341
$65,000	$1,963	$1,512	$1,242	$1,062	$934	$705	$531	$447	$399	$369
$70,000	$2,114	$1,628	$1,337	$1,144	$1,006	$760	$572	$482	$430	$397
$75,000	$2,265	$1,744	$1,433	$1,225	$1,078	$814	$613	$516	$461	$426
$80,000	$2,416	$1,861	$1,528	$1,307	$1,150	$868	$654	$550	$491	$454
$85,000	$2,567	$1,977	$1,624	$1,389	$1,221	$922	$695	$585	$522	$483
$90,000	$2,718	$2,093	$1,719	$1,470	$1,293	$977	$735	$619	$553	$511
$100,000	$3,020	$2,326	$1,910	$1,634	$1,437	$1,085	$817	$688	$614	$568
$125,000	$3,774	$2,907	$2,388	$2,042	$1,796	$1,357	$1,021	$860	$768	$710
$150,000	$4,529	$3,488	$2,865	$2,451	$2,156	$1,628	$1,226	$1,032	$921	$852
$175,000	$5,284	$4,070	$3,343	$2,859	$2,515	$1,899	$1,430	$1,204	$1,075	$994
$200,000	$6,039	$4,651	$3,820	$3,268	$2,874	$2,171	$1,634	$1,376	$1,228	$1,136
$225,000	$6,794	$5,233	$4,298	$3,676	$3,233	$2,442	$1,838	$1,548	$1,382	$1,278
$250,000	$7,549	$5,814	$4,775	$4,084	$3,593	$2,713	$2,043	$1,720	$1,535	$1,419
$275,000	$8,304	$6,396	$5,253	$4,493	$3,952	$2,984	$2,247	$1,892	$1,689	$1,561
$300,000	$9,059	$6,977	$5,730	$4,901	$4,311	$3,256	$2,451	$2,064	$1,842	$1,703

Loan Payment Table

5.75% Rate

Term in Years Amount	3	4	5	6	7	10	15	20	25	30
$1,000	$30	$23	$19	$16	$14	$11	$8	$7	$6	$6
$2,000	$61	$47	$38	$33	$29	$22	$17	$14	$13	$12
$3,000	$91	$70	$58	$49	$43	$33	$25	$21	$19	$18
$4,000	$121	$93	$77	$66	$58	$44	$33	$28	$25	$23
$5,000	$152	$117	$96	$82	$72	$55	$42	$35	$31	$29
$6,000	$182	$140	$115	$99	$87	$66	$50	$42	$38	$35
$7,000	$212	$164	$135	$115	$101	$77	$58	$49	$44	$41
$8,000	$242	$187	$154	$132	$116	$88	$66	$56	$50	$47
$9,000	$273	$210	$173	$148	$130	$99	$75	$63	$57	$53
$10,000	$303	$234	$192	$165	$145	$110	$83	$70	$63	$58
$11,000	$333	$257	$211	$181	$159	$121	$91	$77	$69	$64
$12,000	$364	$280	$231	$197	$174	$132	$100	$84	$75	$70
$13,000	$394	$304	$250	$214	$188	$143	$108	$91	$82	$76
$14,000	$424	$327	$269	$230	$203	$154	$116	$98	$88	$82
$15,000	$455	$351	$288	$247	$217	$165	$125	$105	$94	$88
$16,000	$485	$374	$307	$263	$232	$176	$133	$112	$101	$93
$17,000	$515	$397	$327	$280	$246	$187	$141	$119	$107	$99
$18,000	$546	$421	$346	$296	$261	$198	$149	$126	$113	$105
$19,000	$576	$444	$365	$313	$275	$209	$158	$133	$120	$111
$20,000	$606	$467	$384	$329	$290	$220	$166	$140	$126	$117
$25,000	$758	$584	$480	$411	$362	$274	$208	$176	$157	$146
$30,000	$909	$701	$577	$494	$435	$329	$249	$211	$189	$175
$35,000	$1,061	$818	$673	$576	$507	$384	$291	$246	$220	$204
$40,000	$1,212	$935	$769	$658	$580	$439	$332	$281	$252	$233
$45,000	$1,364	$1,052	$865	$740	$652	$494	$374	$316	$283	$263
$50,000	$1,515	$1,169	$961	$823	$724	$549	$415	$351	$315	$292
$55,000	$1,667	$1,285	$1,057	$905	$797	$604	$457	$386	$346	$321
$60,000	$1,819	$1,402	$1,153	$987	$869	$659	$498	$421	$377	$350
$65,000	$1,970	$1,519	$1,249	$1,070	$942	$713	$540	$456	$409	$379
$70,000	$2,122	$1,636	$1,345	$1,152	$1,014	$768	$581	$491	$440	$409
$75,000	$2,273	$1,753	$1,441	$1,234	$1,087	$823	$623	$527	$472	$438
$80,000	$2,425	$1,870	$1,537	$1,316	$1,159	$878	$664	$562	$503	$467
$85,000	$2,576	$1,986	$1,633	$1,399	$1,232	$933	$706	$597	$535	$496
$90,000	$2,728	$2,103	$1,730	$1,481	$1,304	$988	$747	$632	$566	$525
$100,000	$3,031	$2,337	$1,922	$1,646	$1,449	$1,098	$830	$702	$629	$584
$125,000	$3,789	$2,921	$2,402	$2,057	$1,811	$1,372	$1,038	$878	$786	$729
$150,000	$4,546	$3,506	$2,883	$2,468	$2,173	$1,647	$1,246	$1,053	$944	$875
$175,000	$5,304	$4,090	$3,363	$2,880	$2,536	$1,921	$1,453	$1,229	$1,101	$1,021
$200,000	$6,062	$4,674	$3,843	$3,291	$2,898	$2,195	$1,661	$1,404	$1,258	$1,167
$225,000	$6,819	$5,258	$4,324	$3,702	$3,260	$2,470	$1,868	$1,580	$1,415	$1,313
$250,000	$7,577	$5,843	$4,804	$4,114	$3,622	$2,744	$2,076	$1,755	$1,573	$1,459
$275,000	$8,335	$6,427	$5,285	$4,525	$3,984	$3,019	$2,284	$1,931	$1,730	$1,605
$300,000	$9,093	$7,011	$5,765	$4,937	$4,347	$3,293	$2,491	$2,106	$1,887	$1,751

Loan Payment Table   6.0% Rate

Term in Years	3	4	5	6	7	10	15	20	25	30
Amount										
$1,000	$30	$23	$19	$17	$15	$11	$8	$7	$6	$6
$2,000	$61	$47	$39	$33	$29	$22	$17	$14	$13	$12
$3,000	$91	$70	$58	$50	$44	$33	$25	$21	$19	$18
$4,000	$122	$94	$77	$66	$58	$44	$34	$29	$26	$24
$5,000	$152	$117	$97	$83	$73	$56	$42	$36	$32	$30
$6,000	$183	$141	$116	$99	$88	$67	$51	$43	$39	$36
$7,000	$213	$164	$135	$116	$102	$78	$59	$50	$45	$42
$8,000	$243	$188	$155	$133	$117	$89	$68	$57	$52	$48
$9,000	$274	$211	$174	$149	$131	$100	$76	$64	$58	$54
$10,000	$304	$235	$193	$166	$146	$111	$84	$72	$64	$60
$11,000	$335	$258	$213	$182	$161	$122	$93	$79	$71	$66
$12,000	$365	$282	$232	$199	$175	$133	$101	$86	$77	$72
$13,000	$395	$305	$251	$215	$190	$144	$110	$93	$84	$78
$14,000	$426	$329	$271	$232	$205	$155	$118	$100	$90	$84
$15,000	$456	$352	$290	$249	$219	$167	$127	$107	$97	$90
$16,000	$487	$376	$309	$265	$234	$178	$135	$115	$103	$96
$17,000	$517	$399	$329	$282	$248	$189	$143	$122	$110	$102
$18,000	$548	$423	$348	$298	$263	$200	$152	$129	$116	$108
$19,000	$578	$446	$367	$315	$278	$211	$160	$136	$122	$114
$20,000	$608	$470	$387	$331	$292	$222	$169	$143	$129	$120
$25,000	$761	$587	$483	$414	$365	$278	$211	$179	$161	$150
$30,000	$913	$705	$580	$497	$438	$333	$253	$215	$193	$180
$35,000	$1,065	$822	$677	$580	$511	$389	$295	$251	$226	$210
$40,000	$1,217	$939	$773	$663	$584	$444	$338	$287	$258	$240
$45,000	$1,369	$1,057	$870	$746	$657	$500	$380	$322	$290	$270
$50,000	$1,521	$1,174	$967	$829	$730	$555	$422	$358	$322	$300
$55,000	$1,673	$1,292	$1,063	$912	$803	$611	$464	$394	$354	$330
$60,000	$1,825	$1,409	$1,160	$994	$877	$666	$506	$430	$387	$360
$65,000	$1,977	$1,527	$1,257	$1,077	$950	$722	$549	$466	$419	$390
$70,000	$2,130	$1,644	$1,353	$1,160	$1,023	$777	$591	$502	$451	$420
$75,000	$2,282	$1,761	$1,450	$1,243	$1,096	$833	$633	$537	$483	$450
$80,000	$2,434	$1,879	$1,547	$1,326	$1,169	$888	$675	$573	$515	$480
$85,000	$2,586	$1,996	$1,643	$1,409	$1,242	$944	$717	$609	$548	$510
$90,000	$2,738	$2,114	$1,740	$1,492	$1,315	$999	$759	$645	$580	$540
$100,000	$3,042	$2,349	$1,933	$1,657	$1,461	$1,110	$844	$716	$644	$600
$125,000	$3,803	$2,936	$2,417	$2,072	$1,826	$1,388	$1,055	$896	$805	$749
$150,000	$4,563	$3,523	$2,900	$2,486	$2,191	$1,665	$1,266	$1,075	$966	$899
$175,000	$5,324	$4,110	$3,383	$2,900	$2,556	$1,943	$1,477	$1,254	$1,128	$1,049
$200,000	$6,084	$4,697	$3,867	$3,315	$2,922	$2,220	$1,688	$1,433	$1,289	$1,199
$225,000	$6,845	$5,284	$4,350	$3,729	$3,287	$2,498	$1,899	$1,612	$1,450	$1,349
$250,000	$7,605	$5,871	$4,833	$4,143	$3,652	$2,776	$2,110	$1,791	$1,611	$1,499
$275,000	$8,366	$6,458	$5,317	$4,558	$4,017	$3,053	$2,321	$1,970	$1,772	$1,649
$300,000	$9,127	$7,046	$5,800	$4,972	$4,383	$3,331	$2,532	$2,149	$1,933	$1,799

Loan Payment Table

6.25% Rate

Term in Years Amount	3	4	5	6	7	10	15	20	25	30
$1,000	$31	$24	$19	$17	$15	$11	$9	$7	$7	$6
$2,000	$61	$47	$39	$33	$29	$22	$17	$15	$13	$12
$3,000	$92	$71	$58	$50	$44	$34	$26	$22	$20	$18
$4,000	$122	$94	$78	$67	$59	$45	$34	$29	$26	$25
$5,000	$153	$118	$97	$83	$74	$56	$43	$37	$33	$31
$6,000	$183	$142	$117	$100	$88	$67	$51	$44	$40	$37
$7,000	$214	$165	$136	$117	$103	$79	$60	$51	$46	$43
$8,000	$244	$189	$156	$134	$118	$90	$69	$58	$53	$49
$9,000	$275	$212	$175	$150	$133	$101	$77	$66	$59	$55
$10,000	$305	$236	$194	$167	$147	$112	$86	$73	$66	$62
$11,000	$336	$260	$214	$184	$162	$124	$94	$80	$73	$68
$12,000	$366	$283	$233	$200	$177	$135	$103	$88	$79	$74
$13,000	$397	$307	$253	$217	$191	$146	$111	$95	$86	$80
$14,000	$427	$330	$272	$234	$206	$157	$120	$102	$92	$86
$15,000	$458	$354	$292	$250	$221	$168	$129	$110	$99	$92
$16,000	$489	$378	$311	$267	$236	$180	$137	$117	$106	$99
$17,000	$519	$401	$331	$284	$250	$191	$146	$124	$112	$105
$18,000	$550	$425	$350	$300	$265	$202	$154	$132	$119	$111
$19,000	$580	$448	$370	$317	$280	$213	$163	$139	$125	$117
$20,000	$611	$472	$389	$334	$295	$225	$171	$146	$132	$123
$25,000	$763	$590	$486	$417	$368	$281	$214	$183	$165	$154
$30,000	$916	$708	$583	$501	$442	$337	$257	$219	$198	$185
$35,000	$1,069	$826	$681	$584	$516	$393	$300	$256	$231	$216
$40,000	$1,221	$944	$778	$668	$589	$449	$343	$292	$264	$246
$45,000	$1,374	$1,062	$875	$751	$663	$505	$386	$329	$297	$277
$50,000	$1,527	$1,180	$972	$835	$736	$561	$429	$365	$330	$308
$55,000	$1,679	$1,298	$1,070	$918	$810	$618	$472	$402	$363	$339
$60,000	$1,832	$1,416	$1,167	$1,001	$884	$674	$514	$439	$396	$369
$65,000	$1,985	$1,534	$1,264	$1,085	$957	$730	$557	$475	$429	$400
$70,000	$2,137	$1,652	$1,361	$1,168	$1,031	$786	$600	$512	$462	$431
$75,000	$2,290	$1,770	$1,459	$1,252	$1,105	$842	$643	$548	$495	$462
$80,000	$2,443	$1,888	$1,556	$1,335	$1,178	$898	$686	$585	$528	$493
$85,000	$2,596	$2,006	$1,653	$1,419	$1,252	$954	$729	$621	$561	$523
$90,000	$2,748	$2,124	$1,750	$1,502	$1,326	$1,011	$772	$658	$594	$554
$100,000	$3,054	$2,360	$1,945	$1,669	$1,473	$1,123	$857	$731	$660	$616
$125,000	$3,817	$2,950	$2,431	$2,086	$1,841	$1,404	$1,072	$914	$825	$770
$150,000	$4,580	$3,540	$2,917	$2,504	$2,209	$1,684	$1,286	$1,096	$990	$924
$175,000	$5,344	$4,130	$3,404	$2,921	$2,578	$1,965	$1,500	$1,279	$1,154	$1,078
$200,000	$6,107	$4,720	$3,890	$3,338	$2,946	$2,246	$1,715	$1,462	$1,319	$1,231
$225,000	$6,870	$5,310	$4,376	$3,756	$3,314	$2,526	$1,929	$1,645	$1,484	$1,385
$250,000	$7,634	$5,900	$4,862	$4,173	$3,682	$2,807	$2,144	$1,827	$1,649	$1,539
$275,000	$8,397	$6,490	$5,349	$4,590	$4,050	$3,088	$2,358	$2,010	$1,814	$1,693
$300,000	$9,161	$7,080	$5,835	$5,007	$4,419	$3,368	$2,572	$2,193	$1,979	$1,847

Loan Payment Table   6.50% Rate

Term in Years Amount	3	4	5	6	7	10	15	20	25	30
$1,000	$31	$24	$20	$17	$15	$11	$9	$7	$7	$6
$2,000	$61	$47	$39	$34	$30	$23	$17	$15	$14	$13
$3,000	$92	$71	$59	$50	$45	$34	$26	$22	$20	$19
$4,000	$123	$95	$78	$67	$59	$45	$35	$30	$27	$25
$5,000	$153	$119	$98	$84	$74	$57	$44	$37	$34	$32
$6,000	$184	$142	$117	$101	$89	$68	$52	$45	$41	$38
$7,000	$215	$166	$137	$118	$104	$79	$61	$52	$47	$44
$8,000	$245	$190	$157	$134	$119	$91	$70	$60	$54	$51
$9,000	$276	$213	$176	$151	$134	$102	$78	$67	$61	$57
$10,000	$306	$237	$196	$168	$148	$114	$87	$75	$68	$63
$11,000	$337	$261	$215	$185	$163	$125	$96	$82	$74	$70
$12,000	$368	$285	$235	$202	$178	$136	$105	$89	$81	$76
$13,000	$398	$308	$254	$219	$193	$148	$113	$97	$88	$82
$14,000	$429	$332	$274	$235	$208	$159	$122	$104	$95	$88
$15,000	$460	$356	$293	$252	$223	$170	$131	$112	$101	$95
$16,000	$490	$379	$313	$269	$238	$182	$139	$119	$108	$101
$17,000	$521	$403	$333	$286	$252	$193	$148	$127	$115	$107
$18,000	$552	$427	$352	$303	$267	$204	$157	$134	$122	$114
$19,000	$582	$451	$372	$319	$282	$216	$166	$142	$128	$120
$20,000	$613	$474	$391	$336	$297	$227	$174	$149	$135	$126
$25,000	$766	$593	$489	$420	$371	$284	$218	$186	$169	$158
$30,000	$919	$711	$587	$504	$445	$341	$261	$224	$203	$190
$35,000	$1,073	$830	$685	$588	$520	$397	$305	$261	$236	$221
$40,000	$1,226	$949	$783	$672	$594	$454	$348	$298	$270	$253
$45,000	$1,379	$1,067	$880	$756	$668	$511	$392	$336	$304	$284
$50,000	$1,532	$1,186	$978	$840	$742	$568	$436	$373	$338	$316
$55,000	$1,686	$1,304	$1,076	$925	$817	$625	$479	$410	$371	$348
$60,000	$1,839	$1,423	$1,174	$1,009	$891	$681	$523	$447	$405	$379
$65,000	$1,992	$1,541	$1,272	$1,093	$965	$738	$566	$485	$439	$411
$70,000	$2,145	$1,660	$1,370	$1,177	$1,039	$795	$610	$522	$473	$442
$75,000	$2,299	$1,779	$1,467	$1,261	$1,114	$852	$653	$559	$506	$474
$80,000	$2,452	$1,897	$1,565	$1,345	$1,188	$908	$697	$596	$540	$506
$85,000	$2,605	$2,016	$1,663	$1,429	$1,262	$965	$740	$634	$574	$537
$90,000	$2,758	$2,134	$1,761	$1,513	$1,336	$1,022	$784	$671	$608	$569
$100,000	$3,065	$2,371	$1,957	$1,681	$1,485	$1,135	$871	$746	$675	$632
$125,000	$3,831	$2,964	$2,446	$2,101	$1,856	$1,419	$1,089	$932	$844	$790
$150,000	$4,597	$3,557	$2,935	$2,521	$2,227	$1,703	$1,307	$1,118	$1,013	$948
$175,000	$5,364	$4,150	$3,424	$2,942	$2,599	$1,987	$1,524	$1,305	$1,182	$1,106
$200,000	$6,130	$4,743	$3,913	$3,362	$2,970	$2,271	$1,742	$1,491	$1,350	$1,264
$225,000	$6,896	$5,336	$4,402	$3,782	$3,341	$2,555	$1,960	$1,678	$1,519	$1,422
$250,000	$7,662	$5,929	$4,892	$4,202	$3,712	$2,839	$2,178	$1,864	$1,688	$1,580
$275,000	$8,428	$6,522	$5,381	$4,623	$4,084	$3,123	$2,396	$2,050	$1,857	$1,738
$300,000	$9,195	$7,114	$5,870	$5,043	$4,455	$3,406	$2,613	$2,237	$2,026	$1,896

Loan Payment Table   6.75% Rate

Term in Years Amount	3	4	5	6	7	10	15	20	25	30
$1,000	$31	$24	$20	$17	$15	$11	$9	$8	$7	$6
$2,000	$62	$48	$39	$34	$30	$23	$18	$15	$14	$13
$3,000	$92	$71	$59	$51	$45	$34	$27	$23	$21	$19
$4,000	$123	$95	$79	$68	$60	$46	$35	$30	$28	$26
$5,000	$154	$119	$98	$85	$75	$57	$44	$38	$35	$32
$6,000	$185	$143	$118	$102	$90	$69	$53	$46	$41	$39
$7,000	$215	$167	$138	$119	$105	$80	$62	$53	$48	$45
$8,000	$246	$191	$157	$135	$120	$92	$71	$61	$55	$52
$9,000	$277	$214	$177	$152	$135	$103	$80	$68	$62	$58
$10,000	$308	$238	$197	$169	$150	$115	$88	$76	$69	$65
$11,000	$338	$262	$217	$186	$165	$126	$97	$84	$76	$71
$12,000	$369	$286	$236	$203	$180	$138	$106	$91	$83	$78
$13,000	$400	$310	$256	$220	$195	$149	$115	$99	$90	$84
$14,000	$431	$334	$276	$237	$210	$161	$124	$106	$97	$91
$15,000	$461	$357	$295	$254	$225	$172	$133	$114	$104	$97
$16,000	$492	$381	$315	$271	$240	$184	$142	$122	$111	$104
$17,000	$523	$405	$335	$288	$255	$195	$150	$129	$117	$110
$18,000	$554	$429	$354	$305	$269	$207	$159	$137	$124	$117
$19,000	$584	$453	$374	$322	$284	$218	$168	$144	$131	$123
$20,000	$615	$477	$394	$339	$299	$230	$177	$152	$138	$130
$25,000	$769	$596	$492	$423	$374	$287	$221	$190	$173	$162
$30,000	$923	$715	$591	$508	$449	$344	$265	$228	$207	$195
$35,000	$1,077	$834	$689	$593	$524	$402	$310	$266	$242	$227
$40,000	$1,231	$953	$787	$677	$599	$459	$354	$304	$276	$259
$45,000	$1,384	$1,072	$886	$762	$674	$517	$398	$342	$311	$292
$50,000	$1,538	$1,192	$984	$846	$749	$574	$442	$380	$345	$324
$55,000	$1,692	$1,311	$1,083	$931	$823	$632	$487	$418	$380	$357
$60,000	$1,846	$1,430	$1,181	$1,016	$898	$689	$531	$456	$415	$389
$65,000	$2,000	$1,549	$1,279	$1,100	$973	$746	$575	$494	$449	$422
$70,000	$2,153	$1,668	$1,378	$1,185	$1,048	$804	$619	$532	$484	$454
$75,000	$2,307	$1,787	$1,476	$1,270	$1,123	$861	$664	$570	$518	$486
$80,000	$2,461	$1,906	$1,575	$1,354	$1,198	$919	$708	$608	$553	$519
$85,000	$2,615	$2,026	$1,673	$1,439	$1,273	$976	$752	$646	$587	$551
$90,000	$2,769	$2,145	$1,772	$1,524	$1,347	$1,033	$796	$684	$622	$584
$100,000	$3,076	$2,383	$1,968	$1,693	$1,497	$1,148	$885	$760	$691	$649
$125,000	$3,845	$2,979	$2,460	$2,116	$1,871	$1,435	$1,106	$950	$864	$811
$150,000	$4,614	$3,575	$2,953	$2,539	$2,246	$1,722	$1,327	$1,141	$1,036	$973
$175,000	$5,384	$4,170	$3,445	$2,963	$2,620	$2,009	$1,549	$1,331	$1,209	$1,135
$200,000	$6,153	$4,766	$3,937	$3,386	$2,994	$2,296	$1,770	$1,521	$1,382	$1,297
$225,000	$6,922	$5,362	$4,429	$3,809	$3,368	$2,584	$1,991	$1,711	$1,555	$1,459
$250,000	$7,691	$5,958	$4,921	$4,232	$3,743	$2,871	$2,212	$1,901	$1,727	$1,621
$275,000	$8,460	$6,553	$5,413	$4,656	$4,117	$3,158	$2,434	$2,091	$1,900	$1,784
$300,000	$9,229	$7,149	$5,905	$5,079	$4,491	$3,445	$2,655	$2,281	$2,073	$1,946

Loan Payment Table   7.0% Rate

Term in Years Amount	3	4	5	6	7	10	15	20	25	30
$1,000	$31	$24	$20	$17	$15	$12	$9	$8	$7	$7
$2,000	$62	$48	$40	$34	$30	$23	$18	$16	$14	$13
$3,000	$93	$72	$59	$51	$45	$35	$27	$23	$21	$20
$4,000	$124	$96	$79	$68	$60	$46	$36	$31	$28	$27
$5,000	$154	$120	$99	$85	$75	$58	$45	$39	$35	$33
$6,000	$185	$144	$119	$102	$91	$70	$54	$47	$42	$40
$7,000	$216	$168	$139	$119	$106	$81	$63	$54	$49	$47
$8,000	$247	$192	$158	$136	$121	$93	$72	$62	$57	$53
$9,000	$278	$216	$178	$153	$136	$104	$81	$70	$64	$60
$10,000	$309	$239	$198	$170	$151	$116	$90	$78	$71	$67
$11,000	$340	$263	$218	$188	$166	$128	$99	$85	$78	$73
$12,000	$371	$287	$238	$205	$181	$139	$108	$93	$85	$80
$13,000	$401	$311	$257	$222	$196	$151	$117	$101	$92	$86
$14,000	$432	$335	$277	$239	$211	$163	$126	$109	$99	$93
$15,000	$463	$359	$297	$256	$226	$174	$135	$116	$106	$100
$16,000	$494	$383	$317	$273	$241	$186	$144	$124	$113	$106
$17,000	$525	$407	$337	$290	$257	$197	$153	$132	$120	$113
$18,000	$556	$431	$356	$307	$272	$209	$162	$140	$127	$120
$19,000	$587	$455	$376	$324	$287	$221	$171	$147	$134	$126
$20,000	$618	$479	$396	$341	$302	$232	$180	$155	$141	$133
$25,000	$772	$599	$495	$426	$377	$290	$225	$194	$177	$166
$30,000	$926	$718	$594	$511	$453	$348	$270	$233	$212	$200
$35,000	$1,081	$838	$693	$597	$528	$406	$315	$271	$247	$233
$40,000	$1,235	$958	$792	$682	$604	$464	$360	$310	$283	$266
$45,000	$1,389	$1,078	$891	$767	$679	$522	$404	$349	$318	$299
$50,000	$1,544	$1,197	$990	$852	$755	$581	$449	$388	$353	$333
$55,000	$1,698	$1,317	$1,089	$938	$830	$639	$494	$426	$389	$366
$60,000	$1,853	$1,437	$1,188	$1,023	$906	$697	$539	$465	$424	$399
$65,000	$2,007	$1,557	$1,287	$1,108	$981	$755	$584	$504	$459	$432
$70,000	$2,161	$1,676	$1,386	$1,193	$1,056	$813	$629	$543	$495	$466
$75,000	$2,316	$1,796	$1,485	$1,279	$1,132	$871	$674	$581	$530	$499
$80,000	$2,470	$1,916	$1,584	$1,364	$1,207	$929	$719	$620	$565	$532
$85,000	$2,625	$2,035	$1,683	$1,449	$1,283	$987	$764	$659	$601	$566
$90,000	$2,779	$2,155	$1,782	$1,534	$1,358	$1,045	$809	$698	$636	$599
$100,000	$3,088	$2,395	$1,980	$1,705	$1,509	$1,161	$899	$775	$707	$665
$125,000	$3,860	$2,993	$2,475	$2,131	$1,887	$1,451	$1,124	$969	$883	$832
$150,000	$4,632	$3,592	$2,970	$2,557	$2,264	$1,742	$1,348	$1,163	$1,060	$998
$175,000	$5,403	$4,191	$3,465	$2,984	$2,641	$2,032	$1,573	$1,357	$1,237	$1,164
$200,000	$6,175	$4,789	$3,960	$3,410	$3,019	$2,322	$1,798	$1,551	$1,414	$1,331
$225,000	$6,947	$5,388	$4,455	$3,836	$3,396	$2,612	$2,022	$1,744	$1,590	$1,497
$250,000	$7,719	$5,987	$4,950	$4,262	$3,773	$2,903	$2,247	$1,938	$1,767	$1,663
$275,000	$8,491	$6,585	$5,445	$4,688	$4,150	$3,193	$2,472	$2,132	$1,944	$1,830
$300,000	$9,263	$7,184	$5,940	$5,115	$4,528	$3,483	$2,696	$2,326	$2,120	$1,996

Loan Payment Table   7.50% Rate

Term in Years	3	4	5	6	7	10	15	20	25	30
Amount										
$1,000	$31	$24	$20	$17	$15	$12	$9	$8	$7	$7
$2,000	$62	$48	$40	$35	$31	$24	$19	$16	$15	$14
$3,000	$93	$73	$60	$52	$46	$36	$28	$24	$22	$21
$4,000	$124	$97	$80	$69	$61	$47	$37	$32	$30	$28
$5,000	$156	$121	$100	$86	$77	$59	$46	$40	$37	$35
$6,000	$187	$145	$120	$104	$92	$71	$56	$48	$44	$42
$7,000	$218	$169	$140	$121	$107	$83	$65	$56	$52	$49
$8,000	$249	$193	$160	$138	$123	$95	$74	$64	$59	$56
$9,000	$280	$218	$180	$156	$138	$107	$83	$73	$67	$63
$10,000	$311	$242	$200	$173	$153	$119	$93	$81	$74	$70
$11,000	$342	$266	$220	$190	$169	$131	$102	$89	$81	$77
$12,000	$373	$290	$240	$207	$184	$142	$111	$97	$89	$84
$13,000	$404	$314	$260	$225	$199	$154	$121	$105	$96	$91
$14,000	$435	$339	$281	$242	$215	$166	$130	$113	$103	$98
$15,000	$467	$363	$301	$259	$230	$178	$139	$121	$111	$105
$16,000	$498	$387	$321	$277	$245	$190	$148	$129	$118	$112
$17,000	$529	$411	$341	$294	$261	$202	$158	$137	$126	$119
$18,000	$560	$435	$361	$311	$276	$214	$167	$145	$133	$126
$19,000	$591	$459	$381	$329	$291	$226	$176	$153	$140	$133
$20,000	$622	$484	$401	$346	$307	$237	$185	$161	$148	$140
$25,000	$778	$604	$501	$432	$383	$297	$232	$201	$185	$175
$30,000	$933	$725	$601	$519	$460	$356	$278	$242	$222	$210
$35,000.	$1,089	$846	$701	$605	$537	$415	$324	$282	$259	$245
$40,000	$1,244	$967	$802	$692	$614	$475	$371	$322	$296	$280
$45,000	$1,400	$1,088	$902	$778	$690	$534	$417	$363	$333	$315
$50,000	$1,555	$1,209	$1,002	$865	$767	$594	$464	$403	$369	$350
$55,000	$1,711	$1,330	$1,102	$951	$844	$653	$510	$443	$406	$385
$60,000	$1,866	$1,451	$1,202	$1,037	$920	$712	$556	$483	$443	$420
$65,000	$2,022	$1,572	$1,302	$1,124	$997	$772	$603	$524	$480	$454
$70,000	$2,177	$1,693	$1,403	$1,210	$1,074	$831	$649	$564	$517	$489
$75,000	$2,333	$1,813	$1,503	$1,297	$1,150	$890	$695	$604	$554	$524
$80,000	$2,488	$1,934	$1,603	$1,383	$1,227	$950	$742	$644	$591	$559
$85,000	$2,644	$2,055	$1,703	$1,470	$1,304	$1,009	$788	$685	$628	$594
$90,000	$2,800	$2,176	$1,803	$1,556	$1,380	$1,068	$834	$725	$665	$629
$100,000	$3,111	$2,418	$2,004	$1,729	$1,534	$1,187	$927	$806	$739	$699
$125,000	$3,888	$3,022	$2,505	$2,161	$1,917	$1,484	$1,159	$1,007	$924	$874
$150,000	$4,666	$3,627	$3,006	$2,594	$2,301	$1,781	$1,391	$1,208	$1,108	$1,049
$175,000	$5,444	$4,231	$3,507	$3,026	$2,684	$2,077	$1,622	$1,410	$1,293	$1,224
$200,000	$6,221	$4,836	$4,008	$3,458	$3,068	$2,374	$1,854	$1,611	$1,478	$1,398
$225,000	$6,999	$5,440	$4,509	$3,890	$3,451	$2,671	$2,086	$1,813	$1,663	$1,573
$250,000	$7,777	$6,045	$5,009	$4,323	$3,835	$2,968	$2,318	$2,014	$1,847	$1,748
$275,000	$8,554	$6,649	$5,510	$4,755	$4,218	$3,264	$2,549	$2,215	$2,032	$1,923
$300,000	$9,332	$7,254	$6,011	$5,187	$4,601	$3,561	$2,781	$2,417	$2,217	$2,098

Loan Payment Table 8.0% Rate

Term in Years	3	4	5	6	7	10	15	20	25	30
Amount										
$1,000	$31	$24	$20	$18	$16	$12	$10	$8	$8	$7
$2,000	$63	$49	$41	$35	$31	$24	$19	$17	$15	$15
$3,000	$94	$73	$61	$53	$47	$36	$29	$25	$23	$22
$4,000	$125	$98	$81	$70	$62	$49	$38	$33	$31	$29
$5,000	$157	$122	$101	$88	$78	$61	$48	$42	$39	$37
$6,000	$188	$146	$122	$105	$94	$73	$57	$50	$46	$44
$7,000	$219	$171	$142	$123	$109	$85	$67	$59	$54	$51
$8,000	$251	$195	$162	$140	$125	$97	$76	$67	$62	$59
$9,000	$282	$220	$182	$158	$140	$109	$86	$75	$69	$66
$10,000	$313	$244	$203	$175	$156	$121	$96	$84	$77	$73
$11,000	$345	$269	$223	$193	$171	$133	$105	$92	$85	$81
$12,000	$376	$293	$243	$210	$187	$146	$115	$100	$93	$88
$13,000	$407	$317	$264	$228	$203	$158	$124	$109	$100	$95
$14,000	$439	$342	$284	$245	$218	$170	$134	$117	$108	$103
$15,000	$470	$366	$304	$263	$234	$182	$143	$125	$116	$110
$16,000	$501	$391	$324	$281	$249	$194	$153	$134	$123	$117
$17,000	$533	$415	$345	$298	$265	$206	$162	$142	$131	$125
$18,000	$564	$439	$365	$316	$281	$218	$172	$151	$139	$132
$19,000	$595	$464	$385	$333	$296	$231	$182	$159	$147	$139
$20,000	$627	$488	$406	$351	$312	$243	$191	$167	$154	$147
$25,000	$783	$610	$507	$438	$390	$303	$239	$209	$193	$183
$30,000	$940	$732	$608	$526	$468	$364	$287	$251	$232	$220
$35,000	$1,097	$854	$710	$614	$546	$425	$334	$293	$270	$257
$40,000	$1,253	$977	$811	$701	$623	$485	$382	$335	$309	$294
$45,000	$1,410	$1,099	$912	$789	$701	$546	$430	$376	$347	$330
$50,000	$1,567	$1,221	$1,014	$877	$779	$607	$478	$418	$386	$367
$55,000	$1,724	$1,343	$1,115	$964	$857	$667	$526	$460	$424	$404
$60,000	$1,880	$1,465	$1,217	$1,052	$935	$728	$573	$502	$463	$440
$65,000	$2,037	$1,587	$1,318	$1,140	$1,013	$789	$621	$544	$502	$477
$70,000	$2,194	$1,709	$1,419	$1,227	$1,091	$849	$669	$586	$540	$514
$75,000	$2,350	$1,831	$1,521	$1,315	$1,169	$910	$717	$627	$579	$550
$80,000	$2,507	$1,953	$1,622	$1,403	$1,247	$971	$765	$669	$617	$587
$85,000	$2,664	$2,075	$1,723	$1,490	$1,325	$1,031	$812	$711	$656	$624
$90,000	$2,820	$2,197	$1,825	$1,578	$1,403	$1,092	$860	$753	$695	$660
$100,000	$3,134	$2,441	$2,028	$1,753	$1,559	$1,213	$956	$836	$772	$734
$125,000	$3,917	$3,052	$2,535	$2,192	$1,948	$1,517	$1,195	$1,046	$965	$917
$150,000	$4,700	$3,662	$3,041	$2,630	$2,338	$1,820	$1,433	$1,255	$1,158	$1,101
$175,000	$5,484	$4,272	$3,548	$3,068	$2,728	$2,123	$1,672	$1,464	$1,351	$1,284
$200,000	$6,267	$4,883	$4,055	$3,507	$3,117	$2,427	$1,911	$1,673	$1,544	$1,468
$225,000	$7,051	$5,493	$4,562	$3,945	$3,507	$2,730	$2,150	$1,882	$1,737	$1,651
$250,000	$7,834	$6,103	$5,069	$4,383	$3,897	$3,033	$2,389	$2,091	$1,930	$1,834
$275,000	$8,618	$6,714	$5,576	$4,822	$4,286	$3,337	$2,628	$2,300	$2,122	$2,018
$300,000	$9,401	$7,324	$6,083	$5,260	$4,676	$3,640	$2,867	$2,509	$2,315	$2,201

Loan Payment Table   8.50% Rate

Term in Years	3	4	5	6	7	10	15	20	25	30
Amount										
$1,000	$32	$25	$21	$18	$16	$12	$10	$9	$8	$8
$2,000	$63	$49	$41	$36	$32	$25	$20	$17	$16	$15
$3,000	$95	$74	$62	$53	$48	$37	$30	$26	$24	$23
$4,000	$126	$99	$82	$71	$63	$50	$39	$35	$32	$31
$5,000	$158	$123	$103	$89	$79	$62	$49	$43	$40	$38
$6,000	$189	$148	$123	$107	$95	$74	$59	$52	$48	$46
$7,000	$221	$173	$144	$124	$111	$87	$69	$61	$56	$54
$8,000	$253	$197	$164	$142	$127	$99	$79	$69	$64	$62
$9,000	$284	$222	$185	$160	$143	$112	$89	$78	$72	$69
$10,000	$316	$246	$205	$178	$158	$124	$98	$87	$81	$77
$11,000	$347	$271	$226	$196	$174	$136	$108	$95	$89	$85
$12,000	$379	$296	$246	$213	$190	$149	$118	$104	$97	$92
$13,000	$410	$320	$267	$231	$206	$161	$128	$113	$105	$100
$14,000	$442	$345	$287	$249	$222	$174	$138	$121	$113	$108
$15,000	$474	$370	$308	$267	$238	$186	$148	$130	$121	$115
$16,000	$505	$394	$328	$284	$253	$198	$158	$139	$129	$123
$17,000	$537	$419	$349	$302	$269	$211	$167	$148	$137	$131
$18,000	$568	$444	$369	$320	$285	$223	$177	$156	$145	$138
$19,000	$600	$468	$390	$338	$301	$236	$187	$165	$153	$146
$20,000	$631	$493	$410	$356	$317	$248	$197	$174	$161	$154
$25,000	$789	$616	$513	$444	$396	$310	$246	$217	$201	$192
$30,000	$947	$739	$615	$533	$475	$372	$295	$260	$242	$231
$35,000	$1,105	$863	$718	$622	$554	$434	$345	$304	$282	$269
$40,000	$1,263	$986	$821	$711	$633	$496	$394	$347	$322	$308
$45,000	$1,421	$1,109	$923	$800	$713	$558	$443	$391	$362	$346
$50,000	$1,578	$1,232	$1,026	$889	$792	$620	$492	$434	$403	$384
$55,000	$1,736	$1,356	$1,128	$978	$871	$682	$542	$477	$443	$423
$60,000	$1,894	$1,479	$1,231	$1,067	$950	$744	$591	$521	$483	$461
$65,000	$2,052	$1,602	$1,334	$1,156	$1,029	$806	$640	$564	$523	$500
$70,000	$2,210	$1,725	$1,436	$1,244	$1,109	$868	$689	$607	$564	$538
$75,000	$2,368	$1,849	$1,539	$1,333	$1,188	$930	$739	$651	$604	$577
$80,000	$2,525	$1,972	$1,641	$1,422	$1,267	$992	$788	$694	$644	$615
$85,000	$2,683	$2,095	$1,744	$1,511	$1,346	$1,054	$837	$738	$684	$654
$90,000	$2,841	$2,218	$1,846	$1,600	$1,425	$1,116	$886	$781	$725	$692
$100,000	$3,157	$2,465	$2,052	$1,778	$1,584	$1,240	$985	$868	$805	$769
$125,000	$3,946	$3,081	$2,565	$2,222	$1,980	$1,550	$1,231	$1,085	$1,007	$961
$150,000	$4,735	$3,697	$3,077	$2,667	$2,375	$1,860	$1,477	$1,302	$1,208	$1,153
$175,000	$5,524	$4,313	$3,590	$3,111	$2,771	$2,170	$1,723	$1,519	$1,409	$1,346
$200,000	$6,314	$4,930	$4,103	$3,556	$3,167	$2,480	$1,969	$1,736	$1,610	$1,538
$225,000	$7,103	$5,546	$4,616	$4,000	$3,563	$2,790	$2,216	$1,953	$1,812	$1,730
$250,000	$7,892	$6,162	$5,129	$4,445	$3,959	$3,100	$2,462	$2,170	$2,013	$1,922
$275,000	$8,681	$6,778	$5,642	$4,889	$4,355	$3,410	$2,708	$2,387	$2,214	$2,115
$300,000	$9,470	$7,394	$6,155	$5,334	$4,751	$3,720	$2,954	$2,603	$2,416	$2,307

Loan Payment Table   9.0% Rate

Term in Years	3	4	5	6	7	10	15	20	25	30
Amount										
$1,000	$32	$25	$21	$18	$16	$13	$10	$9	$8	$8
$2,000	$64	$50	$42	$36	$32	$25	$20	$18	$17	$16
$3,000	$95	$75	$62	$54	$48	$38	$30	$27	$25	$24
$4,000	$127	$100	$83	$72	$64	$51	$41	$36	$34	$32
$5,000	$159	$124	$104	$90	$80	$63	$51	$45	$42	$40
$6,000	$191	$149	$125	$108	$97	$76	$61	$54	$50	$48
$7,000	$223	$174	$145	$126	$113	$89	$71	$63	$59	$56
$8,000	$254	$199	$166	$144	$129	$101	$81	$72	$67	$64
$9,000	$286	$224	$187	$162	$145	$114	$91	$81	$76	$72
$10,000	$318	$249	$208	$180	$161	$127	$101	$90	$84	$80
$11,000	$350	$274	$228	$198	$177	$139	$112	$99	$92	$89
$12,000	$382	$299	$249	$216	$193	$152	$122	$108	$101	$97
$13,000	$413	$324	$270	$234	$209	$165	$132	$117	$109	$105
$14,000	$445	$348	$291	$252	$225	$177	$142	$126	$117	$113
$15,000	$477	$373	$311	$270	$241	$190	$152	$135	$126	$121
$16,000	$509	$398	$332	$288	$257	$203	$162	$144	$134	$129
$17,000	$541	$423	$353	$306	$274	$215	$172	$153	$143	$137
$18,000	$572	$448	$374	$324	$290	$228	$183	$162	$151	$145
$19,000	$604	$473	$394	$342	$306	$241	$193	$171	$159	$153
$20,000	$636	$498	$415	$361	$322	$253	$203	$180	$168	$161
$25,000	$795	$622	$519	$451	$402	$317	$254	$225	$210	$201
$30,000	$954	$747	$623	$541	$483	$380	$304	$270	$252	$241
$35,000	$1,113	$871	$727	$631	$563	$443	$355	$315	$294	$282
$40,000	$1,272	$995	$830	$721	$644	$507	$406	$360	$336	$322
$45,000	$1,431	$1,120	$934	$811	$724	$570	$456	$405	$378	$362
$50,000	$1,590	$1,244	$1,038	$901	$804	$633	$507	$450	$420	$402
$55,000	$1,749	$1,369	$1,142	$991	$885	$697	$558	$495	$462	$443
$60,000	$1,908	$1,493	$1,246	$1,082	$965	$760	$609	$540	$504	$483
$65,000	$2,067	$1,618	$1,349	$1,172	$1,046	$823	$659	$585	$545	$523
$70,000	$2,226	$1,742	$1,453	$1,262	$1,126	$887	$710	$630	$587	$563
$75,000	$2,385	$1,866	$1,557	$1,352	$1,207	$950	$761	$675	$629	$603
$80,000	$2,544	$1,991	$1,661	$1,442	$1,287	$1,013	$811	$720	$671	$644
$85,000	$2,703	$2,115	$1,764	$1,532	$1,368	$1,077	$862	$765	$713	$684
$90,000	$2,862	$2,240	$1,868	$1,622	$1,448	$1,140	$913	$810	$755	$724
$100,000	$3,180	$2,489	$2,076	$1,803	$1,609	$1,267	$1,014	$900	$839	$805
$125,000	$3,975	$3,111	$2,595	$2,253	$2,011	$1,583	$1,268	$1,125	$1,049	$1,006
$150,000	$4,770	$3,733	$3,114	$2,704	$2,413	$1,900	$1,521	$1,350	$1,259	$1,207
$175,000	$5,565	$4,355	$3,633	$3,154	$2,816	$2,217	$1,775	$1,575	$1,469	$1,408
$200,000	$6,360	$4,977	$4,152	$3,605	$3,218	$2,534	$2,029	$1,799	$1,678	$1,609
$225,000	$7,155	$5,599	$4,671	$4,056	$3,620	$2,850	$2,282	$2,024	$1,888	$1,810
$250,000	$7,950	$6,221	$5,190	$4,506	$4,022	$3,167	$2,536	$2,249	$2,098	$2,012
$275,000	$8,745	$6,843	$5,709	$4,957	$4,424	$3,484	$2,789	$2,474	$2,308	$2,213
$300,000	$9,540	$7,466	$6,228	$5,408	$4,827	$3,800	$3,043	$2,699	$2,518	$2,414

Loan Payment Table   9.50% Rate

Term in Years	3	4	5	6	7	10	15	20	25	30
Amount										
$1,000	$32	$25	$21	$18	$16	$13	$10	$9	$9	$8
$2,000	$64	$50	$42	$37	$33	$26	$21	$19	$17	$17
$3,000	$96	$75	$63	$55	$49	$39	$31	$28	$26	$25
$4,000	$128	$100	$84	$73	$65	$52	$42	$37	$35	$34
$5,000	$160	$126	$105	$91	$82	$65	$52	$47	$44	$42
$6,000	$192	$151	$126	$110	$98	$78	$63	$56	$52	$50
$7,000	$224	$176	$147	$128	$114	$91	$73	$65	$61	$59
$8,000	$256	$201	$168	$146	$131	$104	$84	$75	$70	$67
$9,000	$288	$226	$189	$164	$147	$116	$94	$84	$79	$76
$10,000	$320	$251	$210	$183	$163	$129	$104	$93	$87	$84
$11,000	$352	$276	$231	$201	$180	$142	$115	$103	$96	$92
$12,000	$384	$301	$252	$219	$196	$155	$125	$112	$105	$101
$13,000	$416	$327	$273	$238	$212	$168	$136	$121	$114	$109
$14,000	$448	$352	$294	$256	$229	$181	$146	$130	$122	$118
$15,000	$480	$377	$315	$274	$245	$194	$157	$140	$131	$126
$16,000	$513	$402	$336	$292	$262	$207	$167	$149	$140	$135
$17,000	$545	$427	$357	$311	$278	$220	$178	$158	$149	$143
$18,000	$577	$452	$378	$329	$294	$233	$188	$168	$157	$151
$19,000	$609	$477	$399	$347	$311	$246	$198	$177	$166	$160
$20,000	$641	$502	$420	$365	$327	$259	$209	$186	$175	$168
$25,000	$801	$628	$525	$457	$409	$323	$261	$233	$218	$210
$30,000	$961	$754	$630	$548	$490	$388	$313	$280	$262	$252
$35,000	$1,121	$879	$735	$640	$572	$453	$365	$326	$306	$294
$40,000	$1,281	$1,005	$840	$731	$654	$518	$418	$373	$349	$336
$45,000	$1,441	$1,131	$945	$822	$735	$582	$470	$419	$393	$378
$50,000	$1,602	$1,256	$1,050	$914	$817	$647	$522	$466	$437	$420
$55,000	$1,762	$1,382	$1,155	$1,005	$899	$712	$574	$513	$481	$462
$60,000	$1,922	$1,507	$1,260	$1,096	$981	$776	$627	$559	$524	$505
$65,000	$2,082	$1,633	$1,365	$1,188	$1,062	$841	$679	$606	$568	$547
$70,000	$2,242	$1,759	$1,470	$1,279	$1,144	$906	$731	$652	$612	$589
$75,000	$2,402	$1,884	$1,575	$1,371	$1,226	$970	$783	$699	$655	$631
$80,000	$2,563	$2,010	$1,680	$1,462	$1,308	$1,035	$835	$746	$699	$673
$85,000	$2,723	$2,135	$1,785	$1,553	$1,389	$1,100	$888	$792	$743	$715
$90,000	$2,883	$2,261	$1,890	$1,645	$1,471	$1,165	$940	$839	$786	$757
$100,000	$3,203	$2,512	$2,100	$1,827	$1,634	$1,294	$1,044	$932	$874	$841
$125,000	$4,004	$3,140	$2,625	$2,284	$2,043	$1,617	$1,305	$1,165	$1,092	$1,051
$150,000	$4,805	$3,768	$3,150	$2,741	$2,452	$1,941	$1,566	$1,398	$1,311	$1,261
$175,000	$5,606	$4,397	$3,675	$3,198	$2,860	$2,264	$1,827	$1,631	$1,529	$1,471
$200,000	$6,407	$5,025	$4,200	$3,655	$3,269	$2,588	$2,088	$1,864	$1,747	$1,682
$225,000	$7,207	$5,653	$4,725	$4,112	$3,677	$2,911	$2,350	$2,097	$1,966	$1,892
$250,000	$8,008	$6,281	$5,250	$4,569	$4,086	$3,235	$2,611	$2,330	$2,184	$2,102
$275,000	$8,809	$6,909	$5,776	$5,026	$4,495	$3,558	$2,872	$2,563	$2,403	$2,312
$300,000	$9,610	$7,537	$6,301	$5,482	$4,903	$3,882	$3,133	$2,796	$2,621	$2,523

Loan Payment Table   10.0% Rate

Term in Years	3	4	5	6	7	10	15	20	25	30
Amount										
$1,000	$32	$25	$21	$19	$17	$13	$11	$10	$9	$9
$2,000	$65	$51	$42	$37	$33	$26	$21	$19	$18	$18
$3,000	$97	$76	$64	$56	$50	$40	$32	$29	$27	$26
$4,000	$129	$101	$85	$74	$66	$53	$43	$39	$36	$35
$5,000	$161	$127	$106	$93	$83	$66	$54	$48	$45	$44
$6,000	$194	$152	$127	$111	$100	$79	$64	$58	$55	$53
$7,000	$226	$178	$149	$130	$116	$93	$75	$68	$64	$61
$8,000	$258	$203	$170	$148	$133	$106	$86	$77	$73	$70
$9,000	$290	$228	$191	$167	$149	$119	$97	$87	$82	$79
$10,000	$323	$254	$212	$185	$166	$132	$107	$97	$91	$88
$11,000	$355	$279	$234	$204	$183	$145	$118	$106	$100	$97
$12,000	$387	$304	$255	$222	$199	$159	$129	$116	$109	$105
$13,000	$419	$330	$276	$241	$216	$172	$140	$125	$118	$114
$14,000	$452	$355	$297	$259	$232	$185	$150	$135	$127	$123
$15,000	$484	$380	$319	$278	$249	$198	$161	$145	$136	$132
$16,000	$516	$406	$340	$296	$266	$211	$172	$154	$145	$140
$17,000	$549	$431	$361	$315	$282	$225	$183	$164	$154	$149
$18,000	$581	$457	$382	$333	$299	$238	$193	$174	$164	$158
$19,000	$613	$482	$404	$352	$315	$251	$204	$183	$173	$167
$20,000	$645	$507	$425	$371	$332	$264	$215	$193	$182	$176
$25,000	$807	$634	$531	$463	$415	$330	$269	$241	$227	$219
$30,000	$968	$761	$637	$556	$498	$396	$322	$290	$273	$263
$35,000	$1,129	$888	$744	$648	$581	$463	$376	$338	$318	$307
$40,000	$1,291	$1,015	$850	$741	$664	$529	$430	$386	$363	$351
$45,000	$1,452	$1,141	$956	$834	$747	$595	$484	$434	$409	$395
$50,000	$1,613	$1,268	$1,062	$926	$830	$661	$537	$483	$454	$439
$55,000	$1,775	$1,395	$1,169	$1,019	$913	$727	$591	$531	$500	$483
$60,000	$1,936	$1,522	$1,275	$1,112	$996	$793	$645	$579	$545	$527
$65,000	$2,097	$1,649	$1,381	$1,204	$1,079	$859	$698	$627	$591	$570
$70,000	$2,259	$1,775	$1,487	$1,297	$1,162	$925	$752	$676	$636	$614
$75,000	$2,420	$1,902	$1,594	$1,389	$1,245	$991	$806	$724	$682	$658
$80,000	$2,581	$2,029	$1,700	$1,482	$1,328	$1,057	$860	$772	$727	$702
$85,000	$2,743	$2,156	$1,806	$1,575	$1,411	$1,123	$913	$820	$772	$746
$90,000	$2,904	$2,283	$1,912	$1,667	$1,494	$1,189	$967	$869	$818	$790
$100,000	$3,227	$2,536	$2,125	$1,853	$1,660	$1,322	$1,075	$965	$909	$878
$125,000	$4,033	$3,170	$2,656	$2,316	$2,075	$1,652	$1,343	$1,206	$1,136	$1,097
$150,000	$4,840	$3,804	$3,187	$2,779	$2,490	$1,982	$1,612	$1,448	$1,363	$1,316
$175,000	$5,647	$4,438	$3,718	$3,242	$2,905	$2,313	$1,881	$1,689	$1,590	$1,536
$200,000	$6,453	$5,073	$4,249	$3,705	$3,320	$2,643	$2,149	$1,930	$1,817	$1,755
$225,000	$7,260	$5,707	$4,781	$4,168	$3,735	$2,973	$2,418	$2,171	$2,045	$1,975
$250,000	$8,067	$6,341	$5,312	$4,631	$4,150	$3,304	$2,687	$2,413	$2,272	$2,194
$275,000	$8,873	$6,975	$5,843	$5,095	$4,565	$3,634	$2,955	$2,654	$2,499	$2,413
$300,000	$9,680	$7,609	$6,374	$5,558	$4,980	$3,965	$3,224	$2,895	$2,726	$2,633

Loan Payment Table   10.50% Rate

Term in Years	3	4	5	6	7	10	15	20	25	30
Amount										
$1,000	$33	$26	$21	$19	$17	$13	$11	$10	$9	$9
$2,000	$65	$51	$43	$38	$34	$27	$22	$20	$19	$18
$3,000	$98	$77	$64	$56	$51	$40	$33	$30	$28	$27
$4,000	$130	$102	$86	$75	$67	$54	$44	$40	$38	$37
$5,000	$163	$128	$107	$94	$84	$67	$55	$50	$47	$46
$6,000	$195	$154	$129	$113	$101	$81	$66	$60	$57	$55
$7,000	$228	$179	$150	$131	$118	$94	$77	$70	$66	$64
$8,000	$260	$205	$172	$150	$135	$108	$88	$80	$76	$73
$9,000	$293	$230	$193	$169	$152	$121	$99	$90	$85	$82
$10,000	$325	$256	$215	$188	$169	$135	$111	$100	$94	$91
$11,000	$358	$282	$236	$207	$185	$148	$122	$110	$104	$101
$12,000	$390	$307	$258	$225	$202	$162	$133	$120	$113	$110
$13,000	$423	$333	$279	$244	$219	$175	$144	$130	$123	$119
$14,000	$455	$358	$301	$263	$236	$189	$155	$140	$132	$128
$15,000	$488	$384	$322	$282	$253	$202	$166	$150	$142	$137
$16,000	$520	$410	$344	$300	$270	$216	$177	$160	$151	$146
$17,000	$553	$435	$365	$319	$287	$229	$188	$170	$161	$156
$18,000	$585	$461	$387	$338	$303	$243	$199	$180	$170	$165
$19,000	$618	$486	$408	$357	$320	$256	$210	$190	$179	$174
$20,000	$650	$512	$430	$376	$337	$270	$221	$200	$189	$183
$25,000	$813	$640	$537	$469	$422	$337	$276	$250	$236	$229
$30,000	$975	$768	$645	$563	$506	$405	$332	$300	$283	$274
$35,000	$1,138	$896	$752	$657	$590	$472	$387	$349	$330	$320
$40,000	$1,300	$1,024	$860	$751	$674	$540	$442	$399	$378	$366
$45,000	$1,463	$1,152	$967	$845	$759	$607	$497	$449	$425	$412
$50,000	$1,625	$1,280	$1,075	$939	$843	$675	$553	$499	$472	$457
$55,000	$1,788	$1,408	$1,182	$1,033	$927	$742	$608	$549	$519	$503
$60,000	$1,950	$1,536	$1,290	$1,127	$1,012	$810	$663	$599	$567	$549
$65,000	$2,113	$1,664	$1,397	$1,221	$1,096	$877	$719	$649	$614	$595
$70,000	$2,275	$1,792	$1,505	$1,315	$1,180	$945	$774	$699	$661	$640
$75,000	$2,438	$1,920	$1,612	$1,408	$1,265	$1,012	$829	$749	$708	$686
$80,000	$2,600	$2,048	$1,720	$1,502	$1,349	$1,079	$884	$799	$755	$732
$85,000	$2,763	$2,176	$1,827	$1,596	$1,433	$1,147	$940	$849	$803	$778
$90,000	$2,925	$2,304	$1,934	$1,690	$1,517	$1,214	$995	$899	$850	$823
$100,000	$3,250	$2,560	$2,149	$1,878	$1,686	$1,349	$1,105	$998	$944	$915
$125,000	$4,063	$3,200	$2,687	$2,347	$2,108	$1,687	$1,382	$1,248	$1,180	$1,143
$150,000	$4,875	$3,841	$3,224	$2,817	$2,529	$2,024	$1,658	$1,498	$1,416	$1,372
$175,000	$5,688	$4,481	$3,761	$3,286	$2,951	$2,361	$1,934	$1,747	$1,652	$1,601
$200,000	$6,500	$5,121	$4,299	$3,756	$3,372	$2,699	$2,211	$1,997	$1,888	$1,829
$225,000	$7,313	$5,761	$4,836	$4,225	$3,794	$3,036	$2,487	$2,246	$2,124	$2,058
$250,000	$8,126	$6,401	$5,373	$4,695	$4,215	$3,373	$2,763	$2,496	$2,360	$2,287
$275,000	$8,938	$7,041	$5,911	$5,164	$4,637	$3,711	$3,040	$2,746	$2,596	$2,516
$300,000	$9,751	$7,681	$6,448	$5,634	$5,058	$4,048	$3,316	$2,995	$2,833	$2,744

Loan Payment Table   11.0% Rate

Term in Years	3	4	5	6	7	10	15	20	25	30
Amount										
$1,000	$33	$26	$22	$19	$17	$14	$11	$10	$10	$10
$2,000	$65	$52	$43	$38	$34	$28	$23	$21	$20	$19
$3,000	$98	$78	$65	$57	$51	$41	$34	$31	$29	$29
$4,000	$131	$103	$87	$76	$68	$55	$45	$41	$39	$38
$5,000	$164	$129	$109	$95	$86	$69	$57	$52	$49	$48
$6,000	$196	$155	$130	$114	$103	$83	$68	$62	$59	$57
$7,000	$229	$181	$152	$133	$120	$96	$80	$72	$69	$67
$8,000	$262	$207	$174	$152	$137	$110	$91	$83	$78	$76
$9,000	$295	$233	$196	$171	$154	$124	$102	$93	$88	$86
$10,000	$327	$258	$217	$190	$171	$138	$114	$103	$98	$95
$11,000	$360	$284	$239	$209	$188	$152	$125	$114	$108	$105
$12,000	$393	$310	$261	$228	$205	$165	$136	$124	$118	$114
$13,000	$426	$336	$283	$247	$223	$179	$148	$134	$127	$124
$14,000	$458	$362	$304	$266	$240	$193	$159	$145	$137	$133
$15,000	$491	$388	$326	$286	$257	$207	$170	$155	$147	$143
$16,000	$524	$414	$348	$305	$274	$220	$182	$165	$157	$152
$17,000	$557	$439	$370	$324	$291	$234	$193	$175	$167	$162
$18,000	$589	$465	$391	$343	$308	$248	$205	$186	$176	$171
$19,000	$622	$491	$413	$362	$325	$262	$216	$196	$186	$181
$20,000	$655	$517	$435	$381	$342	$276	$227	$206	$196	$190
$25,000	$818	$646	$544	$476	$428	$344	$284	$258	$245	$238
$30,000	$982	$775	$652	$571	$514	$413	$341	$310	$294	$286
$35,000	$1,146	$905	$761	$666	$599	$482	$398	$361	$343	$333
$40,000	$1,310	$1,034	$870	$761	$685	$551	$455	$413	$392	$381
$45,000	$1,473	$1,163	$978	$857	$771	$620	$511	$464	$441	$429
$50,000	$1,637	$1,292	$1,087	$952	$856	$689	$568	$516	$490	$476
$55,000	$1,801	$1,422	$1,196	$1,047	$942	$758	$625	$568	$539	$524
$60,000	$1,964	$1,551	$1,305	$1,142	$1,027	$827	$682	$619	$588	$571
$65,000	$2,128	$1,680	$1,413	$1,237	$1,113	$895	$739	$671	$637	$619
$70,000	$2,292	$1,809	$1,522	$1,332	$1,199	$964	$796	$723	$686	$667
$75,000	$2,455	$1,938	$1,631	$1,428	$1,284	$1,033	$852	$774	$735	$714
$80,000	$2,619	$2,068	$1,739	$1,523	$1,370	$1,102	$909	$826	$784	$762
$85,000	$2,783	$2,197	$1,848	$1,618	$1,455	$1,171	$966	$877	$833	$809
$90,000	$2,946	$2,326	$1,957	$1,713	$1,541	$1,240	$1,023	$929	$882	$857
$100,000	$3,274	$2,585	$2,174	$1,903	$1,712	$1,378	$1,137	$1,032	$980	$952
$125,000	$4,092	$3,231	$2,718	$2,379	$2,140	$1,722	$1,421	$1,290	$1,225	$1,190
$150,000	$4,911	$3,877	$3,261	$2,855	$2,568	$2,066	$1,705	$1,548	$1,470	$1,428
$175,000	$5,729	$4,523	$3,805	$3,331	$2,996	$2,411	$1,989	$1,806	$1,715	$1,667
$200,000	$6,548	$5,169	$4,348	$3,807	$3,424	$2,755	$2,273	$2,064	$1,960	$1,905
$225,000	$7,366	$5,815	$4,892	$4,283	$3,853	$3,099	$2,557	$2,322	$2,205	$2,143
$250,000	$8,185	$6,461	$5,436	$4,759	$4,281	$3,444	$2,841	$2,580	$2,450	$2,381
$275,000	$9,003	$7,108	$5,979	$5,234	$4,709	$3,788	$3,126	$2,839	$2,695	$2,619
$300,000	$9,822	$7,754	$6,523	$5,710	$5,137	$4,133	$3,410	$3,097	$2,940	$2,857

Loan Payment Table

11.50% Rate

Term in Years Amount	3	4	5	6	7	10	15	20	25	30
$1,000	$33	$26	$22	$19	$17	$14	$12	$11	$10	$10
$2,000	$66	$52	$44	$39	$35	$28	$23	$21	$20	$20
$3,000	$99	$78	$66	$58	$52	$42	$35	$32	$30	$30
$4,000	$132	$104	$88	$77	$70	$56	$47	$43	$41	$40
$5,000	$165	$130	$110	$96	$87	$70	$58	$53	$51	$50
$6,000	$198	$157	$132	$116	$104	$84	$70	$64	$61	$59
$7,000	$231	$183	$154	$135	$122	$98	$82	$75	$71	$69
$8,000	$264	$209	$176	$154	$139	$112	$93	$85	$81	$79
$9,000	$297	$235	$198	$174	$156	$127	$105	$96	$91	$89
$10,000	$330	$261	$220	$193	$174	$141	$117	$107	$102	$99
$11,000	$363	$287	$242	$212	$191	$155	$129	$117	$112	$109
$12,000	$396	$313	$264	$231	$209	$169	$140	$128	$122	$119
$13,000	$429	$339	$286	$251	$226	$183	$152	$139	$132	$129
$14,000	$462	$365	$308	$270	$243	$197	$164	$149	$142	$139
$15,000	$495	$391	$330	$289	$261	$211	$175	$160	$152	$149
$16,000	$528	$417	$352	$309	$278	$225	$187	$171	$163	$158
$17,000	$561	$444	$374	$328	$296	$239	$199	$181	$173	$168
$18,000	$594	$470	$396	$347	$313	$253	$210	$192	$183	$178
$19,000	$627	$496	$418	$367	$330	$267	$222	$203	$193	$188
$20,000	$660	$522	$440	$386	$348	$281	$234	$213	$203	$198
$25,000	$824	$652	$550	$482	$435	$351	$292	$267	$254	$248
$30,000	$989	$783	$660	$579	$522	$422	$350	$320	$305	$297
$35,000	$1,154	$913	$770	$675	$609	$492	$409	$373	$356	$347
$40,000	$1,319	$1,044	$880	$772	$695	$562	$467	$427	$407	$396
$45,000	$1,484	$1,174	$990	$868	$782	$633	$526	$480	$457	$446
$50,000	$1,649	$1,304	$1,100	$965	$869	$703	$584	$533	$508	$495
$55,000	$1,814	$1,435	$1,210	$1,061	$956	$773	$643	$587	$559	$545
$60,000	$1,979	$1,565	$1,320	$1,157	$1,043	$844	$701	$640	$610	$594
$65,000	$2,143	$1,696	$1,430	$1,254	$1,130	$914	$759	$693	$661	$644
$70,000	$2,308	$1,826	$1,539	$1,350	$1,217	$984	$818	$747	$712	$693
$75,000	$2,473	$1,957	$1,649	$1,447	$1,304	$1,054	$876	$800	$762	$743
$80,000	$2,638	$2,087	$1,759	$1,543	$1,391	$1,125	$935	$853	$813	$792
$85,000	$2,803	$2,218	$1,869	$1,640	$1,478	$1,195	$993	$906	$864	$842
$90,000	$2,968	$2,348	$1,979	$1,736	$1,565	$1,265	$1,051	$960	$915	$891
$100,000	$3,298	$2,609	$2,199	$1,929	$1,739	$1,406	$1,168	$1,066	$1,016	$990
$125,000	$4,122	$3,261	$2,749	$2,411	$2,173	$1,757	$1,460	$1,333	$1,271	$1,238
$150,000	$4,946	$3,913	$3,299	$2,894	$2,608	$2,109	$1,752	$1,600	$1,525	$1,485
$175,000	$5,771	$4,566	$3,849	$3,376	$3,043	$2,460	$2,044	$1,866	$1,779	$1,733
$200,000	$6,595	$5,218	$4,399	$3,858	$3,477	$2,812	$2,336	$2,133	$2,033	$1,981
$225,000	$7,420	$5,870	$4,948	$4,341	$3,912	$3,163	$2,628	$2,399	$2,287	$2,228
$250,000	$8,244	$6,522	$5,498	$4,823	$4,347	$3,515	$2,920	$2,666	$2,541	$2,476
$275,000	$9,068	$7,174	$6,048	$5,305	$4,781	$3,866	$3,213	$2,933	$2,795	$2,723
$300,000	$9,893	$7,827	$6,598	$5,787	$5,216	$4,218	$3,505	$3,199	$3,049	$2,971

Loan Payment Table   12.0% Rate

Term in Years	3	4	5	6	7	10	15	20	25	30
Amount										
$1,000	$33	$26	$22	$20	$18	$14	$12	$11	$11	$10
$2,000	$66	$53	$44	$39	$35	$29	$24	$22	$21	$21
$3,000	$100	$79	$67	$59	$53	$43	$36	$33	$32	$31
$4,000	$133	$105	$89	$78	$71	$57	$48	$44	$42	$41
$5,000	$166	$132	$111	$98	$88	$72	$60	$55	$53	$51
$6,000	$199	$158	$133	$117	$106	$86	$72	$66	$63	$62
$7,000	$233	$184	$156	$137	$124	$100	$84	$77	$74	$72
$8,000	$266	$211	$178	$156	$141	$115	$96	$88	$84	$82
$9,000	$299	$237	$200	$176	$159	$129	$108	$99	$95	$93
$10,000	$332	$263	$222	$196	$177	$143	$120	$110	$105	$103
$11,000	$365	$290	$245	$215	$194	$158	$132	$121	$116	$113
$12,000	$399	$316	$267	$235	$212	$172	$144	$132	$126	$123
$13,000	$432	$342	$289	$254	$229	$187	$156	$143	$137	$134
$14,000	$465	$369	$311	$274	$247	$201	$168	$154	$147	$144
$15,000	$498	$395	$334	$293	$265	$215	$180	$165	$158	$154
$16,000	$531	$421	$356	$313	$282	$230	$192	$176	$169	$165
$17,000	$565	$448	$378	$332	$300	$244	$204	$187	$179	$175
$18,000	$598	$474	$400	$352	$318	$258	$216	$198	$190	$185
$19,000	$631	$500	$423	$371	$335	$273	$228	$209	$200	$195
$20,000	$664	$527	$445	$391	$353	$287	$240	$220	$211	$206
$25,000	$830	$658	$556	$489	$441	$359	$300	$275	$263	$257
$30,000	$996	$790	$667	$587	$530	$430	$360	$330	$316	$309
$35,000	$1,163	$922	$779	$684	$618	$502	$420	$385	$369	$360
$40,000	$1,329	$1,053	$890	$782	$706	$574	$480	$440	$421	$411
$45,000	$1,495	$1,185	$1,001	$880	$794	$646	$540	$495	$474	$463
$50,000	$1,661	$1,317	$1,112	$978	$883	$717	$600	$551	$527	$514
$55,000	$1,827	$1,448	$1,223	$1,075	$971	$789	$660	$606	$579	$566
$60,000	$1,993	$1,580	$1,335	$1,173	$1,059	$861	$720	$661	$632	$617
$65,000	$2,159	$1,712	$1,446	$1,271	$1,147	$933	$780	$716	$685	$669
$70,000	$2,325	$1,843	$1,557	$1,369	$1,236	$1,004	$840	$771	$737	$720
$75,000	$2,491	$1,975	$1,668	$1,466	$1,324	$1,076	$900	$826	$790	$771
$80,000	$2,657	$2,107	$1,780	$1,564	$1,412	$1,148	$960	$881	$843	$823
$85,000	$2,823	$2,238	$1,891	$1,662	$1,500	$1,220	$1,020	$936	$895	$874
$90,000	$2,989	$2,370	$2,002	$1,760	$1,589	$1,291	$1,080	$991	$948	$926
$100,000	$3,321	$2,633	$2,224	$1,955	$1,765	$1,435	$1,200	$1,101	$1,053	$1,029
$125,000	$4,152	$3,292	$2,781	$2,444	$2,207	$1,793	$1,500	$1,376	$1,317	$1,286
$150,000	$4,982	$3,950	$3,337	$2,933	$2,648	$2,152	$1,800	$1,652	$1,580	$1,543
$175,000	$5,813	$4,608	$3,893	$3,421	$3,089	$2,511	$2,100	$1,927	$1,843	$1,800
$200,000	$6,643	$5,267	$4,449	$3,910	$3,531	$2,869	$2,400	$2,202	$2,106	$2,057
$225,000	$7,473	$5,925	$5,005	$4,399	$3,972	$3,228	$2,700	$2,477	$2,370	$2,314
$250,000	$8,304	$6,583	$5,561	$4,888	$4,413	$3,587	$3,000	$2,753	$2,633	$2,572
$275,000	$9,134	$7,242	$6,117	$5,376	$4,855	$3,945	$3,300	$3,028	$2,896	$2,829
$300,000	$9,964	$7,900	$6,673	$5,865	$5,296	$4,304	$3,601	$3,303	$3,160	$3,086

Loan Payment Table   12.50% Rate

Term in Years Amount	3	4	5	6	7	10	15	20	25	30
$1,000	$33	$27	$22	$20	$18	$15	$12	$11	$11	$11
$2,000	$67	$53	$45	$40	$36	$29	$25	$23	$22	$21
$3,000	$100	$80	$67	$59	$54	$44	$37	$34	$33	$32
$4,000	$134	$106	$90	$79	$72	$59	$49	$45	$44	$43
$5,000	$167	$133	$112	$99	$90	$73	$62	$57	$55	$53
$6,000	$201	$159	$135	$119	$108	$88	$74	$68	$65	$64
$7,000	$234	$186	$157	$139	$125	$102	$86	$80	$76	$75
$8,000	$268	$213	$180	$158	$143	$117	$99	$91	$87	$85
$9,000	$301	$239	$202	$178	$161	$132	$111	$102	$98	$96
$10,000	$335	$266	$225	$198	$179	$146	$123	$114	$109	$107
$11,000	$368	$292	$247	$218	$197	$161	$136	$125	$120	$117
$12,000	$401	$319	$270	$238	$215	$176	$148	$136	$131	$128
$13,000	$435	$346	$292	$258	$233	$190	$160	$148	$142	$139
$14,000	$468	$372	$315	$277	$251	$205	$173	$159	$153	$149
$15,000	$502	$399	$337	$297	$269	$220	$185	$170	$164	$160
$16,000	$535	$425	$360	$317	$287	$234	$197	$182	$174	$171
$17,000	$569	$452	$382	$337	$305	$249	$210	$193	$185	$181
$18,000	$602	$478	$405	$357	$323	$263	$222	$205	$196	$192
$19,000	$636	$505	$427	$376	$341	$278	$234	$216	$207	$203
$20,000	$669	$532	$450	$396	$358	$293	$247	$227	$218	$213
$25,000	$836	$664	$562	$495	$448	$366	$308	$284	$273	$267
$30,000	$1,004	$797	$675	$594	$538	$439	$370	$341	$327	$320
$35,000	$1,171	$930	$787	$693	$627	$512	$431	$398	$382	$374
$40,000	$1,338	$1,063	$900	$792	$717	$586	$493	$454	$436	$427
$45,000	$1,505	$1,196	$1,012	$892	$806	$659	$555	$511	$491	$480
$50,000	$1,673	$1,329	$1,125	$991	$896	$732	$616	$568	$545	$534
$55,000	$1,840	$1,462	$1,237	$1,090	$986	$805	$678	$625	$600	$587
$60,000	$2,007	$1,595	$1,350	$1,189	$1,075	$878	$740	$682	$654	$640
$65,000	$2,174	$1,728	$1,462	$1,288	$1,165	$951	$801	$738	$709	$694
$70,000	$2,342	$1,861	$1,575	$1,387	$1,254	$1,025	$863	$795	$763	$747
$75,000	$2,509	$1,993	$1,687	$1,486	$1,344	$1,098	$924	$852	$818	$800
$80,000	$2,676	$2,126	$1,800	$1,585	$1,434	$1,171	$986	$909	$872	$854
$85,000	$2,844	$2,259	$1,912	$1,684	$1,523	$1,244	$1,048	$966	$927	$907
$90,000	$3,011	$2,392	$2,025	$1,783	$1,613	$1,317	$1,109	$1,023	$981	$961
$100,000	$3,345	$2,658	$2,250	$1,981	$1,792	$1,464	$1,233	$1,136	$1,090	$1,067
$125,000	$4,182	$3,322	$2,812	$2,476	$2,240	$1,830	$1,541	$1,420	$1,363	$1,334
$150,000	$5,018	$3,987	$3,375	$2,972	$2,688	$2,196	$1,849	$1,704	$1,636	$1,601
$175,000	$5,854	$4,651	$3,937	$3,467	$3,136	$2,562	$2,157	$1,988	$1,908	$1,868
$200,000	$6,691	$5,316	$4,500	$3,962	$3,584	$2,928	$2,465	$2,272	$2,181	$2,135
$225,000	$7,527	$5,980	$5,062	$4,458	$4,032	$3,293	$2,773	$2,556	$2,453	$2,401
$250,000	$8,363	$6,645	$5,624	$4,953	$4,480	$3,659	$3,081	$2,840	$2,726	$2,668
$275,000	$9,200	$7,309	$6,187	$5,448	$4,928	$4,025	$3,389	$3,124	$2,998	$2,935
$300,000	$10,036	$7,974	$6,749	$5,943	$5,376	$4,391	$3,698	$3,408	$3,271	$3,202

Loan Payment Table   13.0% Rate

Term in Years	3	4	5	6	7	10	15	20	25	30
Amount										
$1,000	$34	$27	$23	$20	$18	$15	$13	$12	$11	$11
$2,000	$67	$54	$46	$40	$36	$30	$25	$23	$23	$22
$3,000	$101	$80	$68	$60	$55	$45	$38	$35	$34	$33
$4,000	$135	$107	$91	$80	$73	$60	$51	$47	$45	$44
$5,000	$168	$134	$114	$100	$91	$75	$63	$59	$56	$55
$6,000	$202	$161	$137	$120	$109	$90	$76	$70	$68	$66
$7,000	$236	$188	$159	$141	$127	$105	$89	$82	$79	$77
$8,000	$270	$215	$182	$161	$146	$119	$101	$94	$90	$88
$9,000	$303	$241	$205	$181	$164	$134	$114	$105	$102	$100
$10,000	$337	$268	$228	$201	$182	$149	$127	$117	$113	$111
$11,000	$371	$295	$250	$221	$200	$164	$139	$129	$124	$122
$12,000	$404	$322	$273	$241	$218	$179	$152	$141	$135	$133
$13,000	$438	$349	$296	$261	$236	$194	$164	$152	$147	$144
$14,000	$472	$376	$319	$281	$255	$209	$177	$164	$158	$155
$15,000	$505	$402	$341	$301	$273	$224	$190	$176	$169	$166
$16,000	$539	$429	$364	$321	$291	$239	$202	$187	$180	$177
$17,000	$573	$456	$387	$341	$309	$254	$215	$199	$192	$188
$18,000	$606	$483	$410	$361	$327	$269	$228	$211	$203	$199
$19,000	$640	$510	$432	$381	$346	$284	$240	$223	$214	$210
$20,000	$674	$537	$455	$401	$364	$299	$253	$234	$226	$221
$25,000	$842	$671	$569	$502	$455	$373	$316	$293	$282	$277
$30,000	$1,011	$805	$683	$602	$546	$448	$380	$351	$338	$332
$35,000	$1,179	$939	$796	$703	$637	$523	$443	$410	$395	$387
$40,000	$1,348	$1,073	$910	$803	$728	$597	$506	$469	$451	$442
$45,000	$1,516	$1,207	$1,024	$903	$819	$672	$569	$527	$508	$498
$50,000.	$1,685	$1,341	$1,138	$1,004	$910	$747	$633	$586	$564	$553
$55,000	$1,853	$1,476	$1,251	$1,104	$1,001	$821	$696	$644	$620	$608
$60,000	$2,022	$1,610	$1,365	$1,204	$1,092	$896	$759	$703	$677	$664
$65,000	$2,190	$1,744	$1,479	$1,305	$1,182	$971	$822	$762	$733	$719
$70,000	$2,359	$1,878	$1,593	$1,405	$1,273	$1,045	$886	$820	$789	$774
$75,000	$2,527	$2,012	$1,706	$1,506	$1,364	$1,120	$949	$879	$846	$830
$80,000	$2,696	$2,146	$1,820	$1,606	$1,455	$1,194	$1,012	$937	$902	$885
$85,000	$2,864	$2,280	$1,934	$1,706	$1,546	$1,269	$1,075	$996	$959	$940
$90,000	$3,032	$2,414	$2,048	$1,807	$1,637	$1,344	$1,139	$1,054	$1,015	$996
$100,000	$3,369	$2,683	$2,275	$2,007	$1,819	$1,493	$1,265	$1,172	$1,128	$1,106
$125,000	$4,212	$3,353	$2,844	$2,509	$2,274	$1,866	$1,582	$1,464	$1,410	$1,383
$150,000	$5,054	$4,024	$3,413	$3,011	$2,729	$2,240	$1,898	$1,757	$1,692	$1,659
$175,000	$5,896	$4,695	$3,982	$3,513	$3,184	$2,613	$2,214	$2,050	$1,974	$1,936
$200,000	$6,739	$5,365	$4,551	$4,015	$3,638	$2,986	$2,530	$2,343	$2,256	$2,212
$225,000	$7,581	$6,036	$5,119	$4,517	$4,093	$3,359	$2,847	$2,636	$2,538	$2,489
$250,000	$8,423	$6,707	$5,688	$5,019	$4,548	$3,733	$3,163	$2,929	$2,820	$2,765
$275,000	$9,266	$7,378	$6,257	$5,520	$5,003	$4,106	$3,479	$3,222	$3,102	$3,042
$300,000	$10,108	$8,048	$6,826	$6,022	$5,458	$4,479	$3,796	$3,515	$3,384	$3,319

Loan Payment Table   13.50% Rate

Term in Years Amount	3	4	5	6	7	10	15	20	25	30
$1,000	$34	$27	$23	$20	$18	$15	$13	$12	$12	$11
$2,000	$68	$54	$46	$41	$37	$30	$26	$24	$23	$23
$3,000	$102	$81	$69	$61	$55	$46	$39	$36	$35	$34
$4,000	$136	$108	$92	$81	$74	$61	$52	$48	$47	$46
$5,000	$170	$135	$115	$102	$92	$76	$65	$60	$58	$57
$6,000	$204	$162	$138	$122	$111	$91	$78	$72	$70	$69
$7,000	$238	$190	$161	$142	$129	$107	$91	$85	$82	$80
$8,000	$271	$217	$184	$163	$148	$122	$104	$97	$93	$92
$9,000	$305	$244	$207	$183	$166	$137	$117	$109	$105	$103
$10,000	$339	$271	$230	$203	$185	$152	$130	$121	$117	$115
$11,000	$373	$298	$253	$224	$203	$168	$143	$133	$128	$126
$12,000	$407	$325	$276	$244	$222	$183	$156	$145	$140	$137
$13,000	$441	$352	$299	$264	$240	$198	$169	$157	$152	$149
$14,000	$475	$379	$322	$285	$259	$213	$182	$169	$163	$160
$15,000	$509	$406	$345	$305	$277	$228	$195	$181	$175	$172
$16,000	$543	$433	$368	$325	$295	$244	$208	$193	$187	$183
$17,000	$577	$460	$391	$346	$314	$259	$221	$205	$198	$195
$18,000	$611	$487	$414	$366	$332	$274	$234	$217	$210	$206
$19,000	$645	$514	$437	$386	$351	$289	$247	$229	$221	$218
$20,000	$679	$542	$460	$407	$369	$305	$260	$241	$233	$229
$25,000	$848	$677	$575	$508	$462	$381	$325	$302	$291	$286
$30,000	$1,018	$812	$690	$610	$554	$457	$389	$362	$350	$344
$35,000	$1,188	$948	$805	$712	$646	$533	$454	$423	$408	$401
$40,000	$1,357	$1,083	$920	$814	$739	$609	$519	$483	$466	$458
$45,000	$1,527	$1,218	$1,035	$915	$831	$685	$584	$543	$525	$515
$50,000	$1,697	$1,354	$1,150	$1,017	$923	$761	$649	$604	$583	$573
$55,000	$1,866	$1,489	$1,266	$1,119	$1,016	$838	$714	$664	$641	$630
$60,000	$2,036	$1,625	$1,381	$1,220	$1,108	$914	$779	$724	$699	$687
$65,000	$2,206	$1,760	$1,496	$1,322	$1,200	$990	$844	$785	$758	$745
$70,000	$2,375	$1,895	$1,611	$1,424	$1,293	$1,066	$909	$845	$816	$802
$75,000	$2,545	$2,031	$1,726	$1,525	$1,385	$1,142	$974	$906	$874	$859
$80,000	$2,715	$2,166	$1,841	$1,627	$1,477	$1,218	$1,039	$966	$933	$916
$85,000	$2,884	$2,301	$1,956	$1,729	$1,570	$1,294	$1,104	$1,026	$991	$974
$90,000	$3,054	$2,437	$2,071	$1,831	$1,662	$1,370	$1,168	$1,087	$1,049	$1,031
$100,000	$3,394	$2,708	$2,301	$2,034	$1,846	$1,523	$1,298	$1,207	$1,166	$1,145
$125,000	$4,242	$3,385	$2,876	$2,542	$2,308	$1,903	$1,623	$1,509	$1,457	$1,432
$150,000	$5,090	$4,061	$3,451	$3,051	$2,770	$2,284	$1,947	$1,811	$1,748	$1,718
$175,000	$5,939	$4,738	$4,027	$3,559	$3,231	$2,665	$2,272	$2,113	$2,040	$2,004
$200,000	$6,787	$5,415	$4,602	$4,068	$3,693	$3,045	$2,597	$2,415	$2,331	$2,291
$225,000	$7,635	$6,092	$5,177	$4,576	$4,155	$3,426	$2,921	$2,717	$2,623	$2,577
$250,000	$8,484	$6,769	$5,752	$5,085	$4,616	$3,807	$3,246	$3,018	$2,914	$2,864
$275,000	$9,332	$7,446	$6,328	$5,593	$5,078	$4,188	$3,570	$3,320	$3,206	$3,150
$300,000	$10,181	$8,123	$6,903	$6,102	$5,539	$4,568	$3,895	$3,622	$3,497	$3,436

Loan Payment Table   14.0% Rate

Term in Years Amount	3	4	5	6	7	10	15	20	25	30
$1,000	$34	$27	$23	$21	$19	$16	$13	$12	$12	$12
$2,000	$68	$55	$47	$41	$37	$31	$27	$25	$24	$24
$3,000	$103	$82	$70	$62	$56	$47	$40	$37	$36	$36
$4,000	$137	$109	$93	$82	$75	$62	$53	$50	$48	$47
$5,000	$171	$137	$116	$103	$94	$78	$67	$62	$60	$59
$6,000	$205	$164	$140	$124	$112	$93	$80	$75	$72	$71
$7,000	$239	$191	$163	$144	$131	$109	$93	$87	$84	$83
$8,000	$273	$219	$186	$165	$150	$124	$107	$99	$96	$95
$9,000	$308	$246	$209	$185	$169	$140	$120	$112	$108	$107
$10,000	$342	$273	$233	$206	$187	$155	$133	$124	$120	$118
$11,000	$376	$301	$256	$227	$206	$171	$146	$137	$132	$130
$12,000	$410	$328	$279	$247	$225	$186	$160	$149	$144	$142
$13,000	$444	$355	$302	$268	$244	$202	$173	$162	$156	$154
$14,000	$478	$383	$326	$288	$262	$217	$186	$174	$169	$166
$15,000	$513	$410	$349	$309	$281	$233	$200	$187	$181	$178
$16,000	$547	$437	$372	$330	$300	$248	$213	$199	$193	$190
$17,000	$581	$465	$396	$350	$319	$264	$226	$211	$205	$201
$18,000	$615	$492	$419	$371	$337	$279	$240	$224	$217	$213
$19,000	$649	$519	$442	$392	$356	$295	$253	$236	$229	$225
$20,000	$684	$547	$465	$412	$375	$311	$266	$249	$241	$237
$25,000	$854	$683	$582	$515	$469	$388	$333	$311	$301	$296
$30,000	$1,025	$820	$698	$618	$562	$466	$400	$373	$361	$355
$35,000	$1,196	$956	$814	$721	$656	$543	$466	$435	$421	$415
$40,000	$1,367	$1,093	$931	$824	$750	$621	$533	$497	$482	$474
$45,000	$1,538	$1,230	$1,047	$927	$843	$699	$599	$560	$542	$533
$50,000	$1,709	$1,366	$1,163	$1,030	$937	$776	$666	$622	$602	$592
$55,000	$1,880	$1,503	$1,280	$1,133	$1,031	$854	$732	$684	$662	$652
$60,000	$2,051	$1,640	$1,396	$1,236	$1,124	$932	$799	$746	$722	$711
$65,000	$2,222	$1,776	$1,512	$1,339	$1,218	$1,009	$866	$808	$782	$770
$70,000	$2,392	$1,913	$1,629	$1,442	$1,312	$1,087	$932	$870	$843	$829
$75,000	$2,563	$2,049	$1,745	$1,545	$1,406	$1,164	$999	$933	$903	$889
$80,000	$2,734	$2,186	$1,861	$1,648	$1,499	$1,242	$1,065	$995	$963	$948
$85,000	$2,905	$2,323	$1,978	$1,751	$1,593	$1,320	$1,132	$1,057	$1,023	$1,007
$90,000	$3,076	$2,459	$2,094	$1,855	$1,687	$1,397	$1,199	$1,119	$1,083	$1,066
$100,000	$3,418	$2,733	$2,327	$2,061	$1,874	$1,553	$1,332	$1,244	$1,204	$1,185
$125,000	$4,272	$3,416	$2,909	$2,576	$2,343	$1,941	$1,665	$1,554	$1,505	$1,481
$150,000	$5,127	$4,099	$3,490	$3,091	$2,811	$2,329	$1,998	$1,865	$1,806	$1,777
$175,000	$5,981	$4,782	$4,072	$3,606	$3,280	$2,717	$2,331	$2,176	$2,107	$2,074
$200,000	$6,836	$5,465	$4,654	$4,121	$3,748	$3,105	$2,663	$2,487	$2,408	$2,370
$225,000	$7,690	$6,148	$5,235	$4,636	$4,217	$3,493	$2,996	$2,798	$2,708	$2,666
$250,000	$8,544	$6,832	$5,817	$5,151	$4,685	$3,882	$3,329	$3,109	$3,009	$2,962
$275,000	$9,399	$7,515	$6,399	$5,667	$5,154	$4,270	$3,662	$3,420	$3,310	$3,258
$300,000	$10,253	$8,198	$6,980	$6,182	$5,622	$4,658	$3,995	$3,731	$3,611	$3,555

Order Form

#	Title	Investment per	Total amount
_____	**It's Your Money! Tools, tips and tricks to borrow smarter & pay it off quicker**	**$ 14.95**	_____
_____	Colorful Personalities – Discover Your Personality Type Through the Power of Colors	$ 14.95	_____
_____	The Colors of Leadership and Management booklet	$ 4.90	_____
_____	The Colors of Parent and Child Dynamics booklet	$ 4.90	_____
_____	The Colors of Sales and Customers booklet	$ 4.90	_____
_____	The Colors of Relationships booklet	$ 4.90	_____
_____	Any four booklets package	$ 14.95	_____
_____	Colorful Personalities – Audio CD	$ 9.95	_____

Sales Tax   **no charge**
Postage (flat amount)   **$ 4.00**

Total amount: _____

Payment and mailing information:

Name: _____

Address: _____

City: _____ State: _____ Zip: _____

E-mail: _____

Payment enclosed by: _____check _____cash _____money order, or

    Visa/MC: _____/_____/_____/_____ Expiry date:_____/_____

Order by: Fax: (780) 432 5613
         E-mail: sales@yourmoneybook.com
         Mail: Suite 1183 - 14781 Memorial Dr., Houston, TX 77079